The Mentoring Manual

The Mentoring Manual

Mike Whittaker
and
Ann Cartwright

Gower

Published by
Gower Publishing Limited
Gower House
Croft Road
Aldershot
Hampshire GU11 3HR
England

Gower Publishing Company
131 Main Street
Burlington VT 05401-5600 USA

Reprinted 2002

British Library Cataloguing in Publication Data
Whittaker, Mike, 1944–
  The mentoring manual
  1. Mentoring in business
  I. Title II. Cartwright, Ann, 1953–
  658.3'124

ISBN 0 566 08147 4

Library of Congress Cataloging-in-Publication Data
Whittaker, Mike, 1944–
    The mentoring manual / Mike Whittaker and Ann Cartwright.
      p. cm.
    Includes index.
    ISBN 0-566-08147-4
    1. Mentoring in business—Handbooks, manuals, etc. 2. Mentoring in the
professions—Handbooks, manuals, etc. I. Cartwright, Ann, 1953– II. Title.

HF5385.W48 2000
658.3'124—dc21   99-049656

Typeset in 11 point Times by Bournemouth Colour Press, Parkstone and printed in Great Britain by MPG Books Ltd, Bodmin.

Contents

List of forms

List of OHP transparency copies

Preface

Writing a book is really hard work, for me at least. So, there must be a reason why I was prepared to sit down and write a second one on the same subject. I asked Ann what she felt and she agreed there was a lot to explore and write on mentoring. Julia Scott and Jonathan Norman of Gower were incredibly helpful and encouraging and the project got underway in 1998, a year which was for me both difficult and challenging. This book – or manual, I'll leave you to judge what is the most appropriate description – has been based on review of some existing schemes, our own mentoring experiences and reference to publications, both books and articles. We are grateful to people who were prepared to give us time to discuss their mentoring experiences with us.

None of this really answers my original question about why I should want to write another book on mentoring. I could say, 'It's a really fascinating subject, it's definitely here to stay and it fits in with my own approach and experiences as a trainer to help people learn.' That's all true but I have two examples, the difference between which I think illustrates why I really like the subject and why I wanted to write something else on it.

In the 1990s I worked for a highly successful training organization that delivered programmes to a whole range of 'blue chip' companies in various sectors. Much of the material used hadn't changed in twenty years, but clients continued to invest in some very expensive training because the programmes were expertly delivered and relevant to their needs. (Incidentally, you can take me out of the equation of 'expert' because this wasn't the job for me nor did I suit the organization.) In spite of a heavy investment in training of this nature, I'm not all that convinced that much of it was ever put into practice. I can't blame the training organization for this. It was very much down to the clients. As for coaching and mentoring, the organization suggested they were interested but I never saw any real evidence of this.

My second example occurred in 1998. As part of research for this book I went to Kimberworth School in Rotherham to review their experience of a mentoring scheme for some 14–15 year-old children. This was part of an education/business initiative aimed at Rotherham schools, which received limited European funding. I had the opportunity to meet some of the children, mentors and mentoring support staff at the school. It was very rewarding to hear how eloquently the children described their experiences. It was very much a case of 'before' and 'after'. The mentors and staff said, 'You should have seen them twelve months ago; they wouldn't have said boo to a goose. Their self-esteem is much higher and they believe in themselves, as you can see for yourself.'

So, I believe in mentoring because it can contribute so much to self-belief and it's a subject I'm prepared to invest considerable time in writing about. It can happen either informally or formally. It doesn't necessarily cost a fortune to put in place, and you can often anticipate significant benefits to those involved. On the other hand, your organization might be prepared to invest heavily in training or consultancy and at the end of the day you may be left wondering what you have got for your money. I'm sure you've come across this before.

I wonder what Ann will say after I've said all this!

Since writing the last book with Mike I have spent a varying amount of time and energy exploring and developing mentoring and co-mentoring relationships for myself and others. In addition, I have been directly involved in mentoring two people, both of whom have gone on to bigger and better things.

My real passion on this subject at the moment is *co-mentoring*, especially for chief executives and senior managers and those managers who are very isolated in their workplace because of location or because they happen to be the only woman or black person in a senior position within their organization.

I am particularly interested in how mentoring can be used to promote self-development and how it can be used to manage the process of change, and I have included some thoughts on both these areas in Chapter 6.

Writers' contact addresses

One of the themes in our book is how important it is to be receptive to learning at any time. To increase our learning and knowledge we would appreciate readers' reactions to the book and feedback on the progress of their individual mentoring schemes.

We can be contacted as follows:

Mike Whittaker
5 Belford Drive, Bramley, Rotherham, S66 3YW
Tel: 01709 545691
E-mail – MWhitt1610@AOL.com

Ann Cartwright
18 Ann Potter Close, Ockbrook, Derbyshire, DE72 3TD
Tel: 01322 664605
E-mail – Ann.Cartwright@btinternet.com

Mike Whittaker
Ann Cartwright

Acknowledgements

We would like to thank the following people who have helped us during the project:

Bob McGeachie and Joan Fallows for providing useful insights on the Sheffield headteacher programme.

The headteachers themselves who were prepared to give their time to be interviewed. Their enthusiasm must be a significant reason why the scheme has been successful.

Derek Ainscough from Business Education Links and the staff and pupils of Kimberworth School, particularly Carol Wilson and Howard Thomas.

Mark Napper and Derek Powell who are involved in the very interesting Wakefield and Pontefract GP scheme.

All the employees at the Sheffield site of Fort James UK where Mike Whittaker spent a lot of time from May 1998 to May 1999.

All the people who completed questionnaires as part of the organizational case study.

All the Voluntary Sector Women Managers who helped Ann Cartwright by contributing their thoughts on mentoring, especially her own co-mentor.

People who are taking part in the co-mentoring initiative especially the local TEC for their contribution and support.

MW
AC

Chapter 1

Introduction

As with our previous book, we start by trying to imagine who you, the reader, are. Later on we will consider the different roles associated with mentoring. Our initial guess is that you have an important part to play in either starting up a new scheme or you wish to review the one that you've already got. We may have this totally wrong. You may have picked up this book through idle curiosity and are thinking, 'Another book on mentoring. What's different about this one?' We start with a few words of caution based on our experiences of attempting to wade through what could be loosely termed 'business books'.

Don't read this book from cover to cover. If you want to do that, go and buy yourself a contemporary novel. You'll enjoy this book much more and hopefully get something out of it if you *pick and mix*.

Below, we will talk about the main sections and include some guidance notes to help you find your way around. It is a little bit different in style from our previous book, *32 Activities on Coaching and Mentoring*, in that there is more narrative this time. If you have a pivotal role in mentoring there should be a place on your shelf for both books.

The first manual was very much aimed at developing skills with activities which you could use yourself or make available to others. This book is very much concerned with the actual implementation of mentoring but with frequent reference to the skill element. If you're looking for something fairly comprehensive on mentoring you've come to the right place.

Going back to your possible needs from a book like this, we think that you are looking for something which:

● helps you understand what practical mentoring is all about
● you feel like reading
● you can lend to others
● is a new source of ideas
● is not too full of trainer-speak
● has material that you can copy legally
● helps you set up a mentoring programme

- helps you review what we've already got
- is easy to find your way around
- answers the question, 'Why should we bother with mentoring here?'
- contains some ammunition to convince others
- is a comprehensive guide on mentoring
- has a logical structure
- contains the material you need
- has good examples and illustrations
- is concise and not too wordy
- considers the various mentoring roles (and those not immediately involved)
- considers the development of both mentors and mentees
- doesn't assume that everybody thinks it's the best thing since sliced bread
- provides me with some ideas to solve difficult problems
- can be used alongside other initiatives
- helps you to sell mentoring to others
- provides the answer to whether or not you should become a mentor.

This seems a very long list but there may be others we haven't thought about. We hope there is something here relevant to you.

Now we will briefly discuss the chapters in this manual.

Chapter 1   Introduction

In this first chapter we consider some of the issues relevant to mentoring in general, including the wide application and the benefits.

Chapter 2   Mentoring in operation

The two writers carried out studies in a number of organizations, which currently have mentoring schemes. This resulted in useful discussion with participants in the schemes and also facilitators/administrators. While no one scheme is the same as any other, we were able to identify some key learning features worth taking into account for readers who are currently planning to implement a scheme in their own organization.

Chapter 3   Practical considerations

We would claim this to be the most weighty and most significant part of the book. The first part looks at what we consider to be the most important aspects of successful, and for that matter unsuccessful, mentoring. There will inevitably be some overlap in the sections, but hopefully the reader will appreciate that we have aimed for consistency. This section combines our thoughts on the practical aspects of mentoring and some activities which readers can try for themselves. It will never be all plain sailing and there are examples of either situation which are difficult or those where things simply go wrong.

The second part of the chapter considers the mentoring relationship. It is a bit like an outsider looking in. In practice this could be the facilitator, almost like a guardian angel wanting to offer help on the process if needed but not actually getting involved in the detail. Effective mentoring involves discretion, privacy and trust. The effective facilitator is aware of the delicate balance needed between contributing to a first-class mentoring scheme by learning from various mentoring relationships but still remaining the soul of discretion. It sounds quite difficult, doesn't it?

In the third part we try to encompass effective mentoring with a limited number of key learning points. This could help you if, when running a course or workshop somebody comes up to you and says, 'I'm thinking of setting up a mentoring scheme. What are the few things I have to do to make sure it's a success?'

Chapter 4   Taking action

The previous chapter has got you thinking what you would like to do. This one provides you with some material to take it a step further. At the end of a course or workshop, individual action plans are usually agreed. If you are the tutor or course leader, you may wonder if anything different will actually happen when delegates return to their normal job. As the writers of this manual, we are in a similar position. Hopefully, the material is of sufficient interest to ensure you will do something different or look at mentoring in a new light.

Chapter 5   Developing mentoring skills

This is a section to help you develop mentoring skills in your organization or assist you in your own self-development. We revisit some of the material from our previous book but in less depth this time. Some examples of our own experiences, both as trainers and delegates, are included.

Chapter 6   Writers' personal reflections

This includes some extracts which candidly illustrate our learning, both as mentors and trainers.

Guidance on using the sections

How you choose to use the manual will depend on your previous experience of mentoring. If your organization has a scheme already in place, you may want to focus on the trouble-shooting aspects. For example, you may feel your scheme is not getting the support it needs from line managers. In Chapter 3, section 11, one of the examples given, 'Adverse reactions to mentoring from a line manager' (Problem Area 2), presents you with some ideas on how you might wish to tackle this situation.

On the other hand, you might only be at the stage of considering whether or not your organization needs a formal mentoring scheme. In this case you might look through the examples in Chapter 2. This will give you an indication of the sort of learning processes these organizations have gone through. Then home in on your own organization and review the 11 sections, selecting those parts which are of most value to you. It is worth remembering that you will need the full co-operation of others if you are to have a successful scheme. If it helps to get people on board, copy sections, forms or examples and pass these on to your colleagues.

Applications, definitions and benefits

Applications

In the course of this book we will cover a whole range of situations where some form or other of mentoring has been applied. If we don't mention the original Greek origin of the word (after this initial reference) this is because this seems to be how every book on the subject begins. It's worth making the point straightaway that, although you may be reading this manual now because of your interest in a variation on a formal scheme, informal mentoring can take place in all sorts of guises.

In Chapter 3 we talk about formal and informal mentoring in more depth. While most of the material here focuses on the formal approach, hopefully there will be things here to help you if you simply want some ideas on informal mentoring.

Definitions

This is what we said in our first book on the subject, *32 Activities on Coaching and Mentoring*, a definition which we borrowed from a friend of ours, Dave Megginson:

> 'Providing guidance, support and practical help through life crises or into new stages of development.'

It is three years since we finished writing the other book; three years in which we have delved into a number of schemes as researchers; three years when we have also directly increased our experience as mentors. We like that original definition and see no reason to try to re-define it. There is a postscript and this comes as a result of our research. While this is not so much a definition but more a purpose, Rosie Firth, headteacher at Brunswick School in Sheffield suggested: Mentoring: 'So they can stand alone.' The 'they' referred to mentees. We like this but also wonder if in some way the 'they' could apply to mentors as well. This is an opportune moment to consider who can actually benefit from mentoring.

Benefits

Assuming we are considering a formal application of mentoring, potential benefits can be gained by:

- mentees
- mentors
- the organization.

Examples of possible benefits:

Mentee

- increased confidence as a result of personal achievement
- others appreciate and value the mentee's hidden potential
- has new targets to aim for.

Mentor

- highlights the mentor's potential
- others see you in a more favourable light
- gains personal satisfaction as a result of being an effective mentor.

Organization

- Mentoring can provide support to other initiatives (such as management development).
- It can lead to improved individual and team performance.
- It can assist the implementation of change.

In the course of our studies of existing mentoring schemes we came across some other very interesting ones:

Mentees

1   'She had doubts as to whether she could really do the job. After mentoring, she knew she could do it.'
2   'It rescued him from a disaster.'

Mentors

1   'It's given me a clearer vision about my current job.'
2   'Now I plan more effectively.'

Organization

1   'It's reduced labour turnover.'
2   'It provided the school with the opportunity to show parents there was a potential problem, while offering a possible solution.'

In Chapter 3 the various participants in mentoring are discussed at some length. To the roles of mentee and mentors can be added: facilitator/administrator (this could be you), champion/sponsor and line manager. We think there are potential benefits to be gained for these other key players. Influencing others is regarded as a significant consideration in contributing to a successful mentoring scheme. If your role necessitates your 'selling' mentoring to others you may want to draw up your own list of possible benefits.

Cautionary words

We don't wish to appear too negative in our introduction, but think you should keep your two feet on the ground when it comes to convincing others about the advantages of mentoring. The following may not apply to you but if they do think carefully about your strategy:

Case 1

If you need your scheme to be funded from outside your organization, don't think for one minute that those involved will have a clue what mentoring is all about. From some quarters you might also expect, 'What are the quantifiable outcomes expected from your mentoring proposal?' This often comes from someone who works for an organization where quantifiable outcomes apply to others but somehow not their own organization.

Case 2

People will sometimes talk about 'mentoring' but in practice what they are talking about is nothing of the sort. Some national initiatives fall into this category. This adds to general confusion.

Case 3

There are others who will 'talk a good game'. This is the story of all those initiatives confined very swiftly to the wastepaper bin. 'We've had mentoring in here for five years. It works well.' Then you check and find it started out full of promise, like 'total quality' and 'appraisal', but soon fell by the wayside. This may sound as though it runs counter to our suggestion that the use of mentoring is becoming more extensive. Our word of caution is to remind you that things might not be always as they seem. It is easy to be drawn into the situation of starting but never finishing. The writers wanted to develop this theme in an article for a well-known management magazine but there didn't seem to be any interest. 'We're more interested in actual case studies rather than general themes.' By this we understood them to mean they only wanted the usual collection of 'success stories' which soon seem to go the same way as some of the 'excellent' companies from *In Search of Excellence* (see References and Recommended Reading).

About successful learning

We appreciate that the breadth of experience of mentoring and learning among our readers will vary considerably. You, the reader, will not agree with everything we say. If you have tried something out and it's worked well, in spite of what others have said, quite rightly you'll chose to stick with it. We can also be pragmatic and will occasionally describe our favourite theories and models, which again have worked for us.

Two theories we feel particularly appropriate for mentoring are:

- the Kolb Learning Cycle
- the Johari Window.

The latter, with which you may already be familiar, encourages both self-awareness and can be a catalyst for personal change.

The Kolb Learning Cycle (an adaptation)

In order for successful learning to take place, the learner needs to go through a four-stage process:

1 Action
2 Reflection
3 Conclusion
4 Planning.

By systematically and consciously going through each of the four stages, the learner is able to:

- recognize and reinforce behaviours and actions that worked well
- identify how and why behaviours and actions failed
- identify and change the behaviours and actions to prevent similar failure in the future
- learn from mistakes and success.

However, all too often, people fail to take themselves through all four stages and as a result very often fail to learn from their mistakes and failures. Instead they practise the 'action-reflection bounce'.

What is the action-reflection bounce?

The action-reflection bounce is the process that, in our view, more people go through instead of using the four-stage learning cycle. It works in the following way:

- During the day something happens that makes us stop and think – the *action*.
- At some later point (e.g. immediately after the event; on our way home; tossing and turning at night) we ponder and reflect on the events of the day, our behaviours and actions and their impact on others – the *reflection*.
- *Then we forget about it.*

True, we may have drawn some conclusions from the event and identified things that could have been done differently or better. But, in reality, most of us fail to draw any real conclusions and almost never really plan how we will do things differently or better next time around. So when a similar situation arises in the future we behave and act in the same ways and usually achieve the same results. We then go through the same reflection process and so we go on doing the action-reflection bounce! In short, we *don't learn from our mistakes*.

The mentoring process is an ideal way to stop the action-reflection bounce and begin to develop the *learning roll*.

What is the learning roll and how can mentoring help?

The learning roll is the four-stage process described earlier and illustrated below.

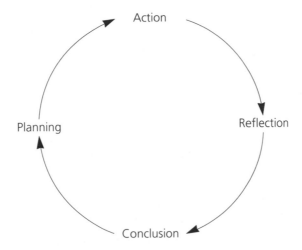

It is a cyclical process that helps people to systematically and consciously move around the cycle. Hence, the 'learning roll' – to really learn you need to roll round the four stages.

In the mentoring process, a skilled mentor will help the mentee to 'roll' around the four stages and therefore maximize their learning potential. Each mentoring session can be structured to ensure that the learning roll is actively used and continuously reviewed.

The learning roll can also be used as the framework to carry out regular reviews of the mentoring process to ensure that it is still meeting the needs of both the mentor and the mentee.

How we have used the learning roll in this book

The chapters in this book are designed to help the reader to move through the learning roll by:

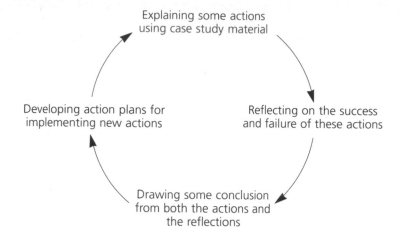

See the OHP transparency copy opposite.

We have collected and written a number of case studies drawn from a cross-section of organizations. We will use these to highlight and identify:

- The common learning themes that can be drawn from each example.
- The features that are present in a successful mentoring scheme.
- The benefits that can be gained from a mentoring scheme both at an individual level and at a personal level.
- The pitfalls to try to avoid when setting up a mentoring scheme.
- The skills required by successful mentors.

We will be linking into our earlier publication, *32 Activities on Coaching and Mentoring* to provide ideas for developing the skills of both mentors and mentees as well as giving you some ideas about structuring these activities in workshop sessions.

We hope this manual will help you to gain more insights into the benefits and features of the mentoring process, and that the style and format will help you to successfully complete the 'learning roll' and that this in turn will help you to successfully introduce and implement mentoring within your own organization.

The learning roll

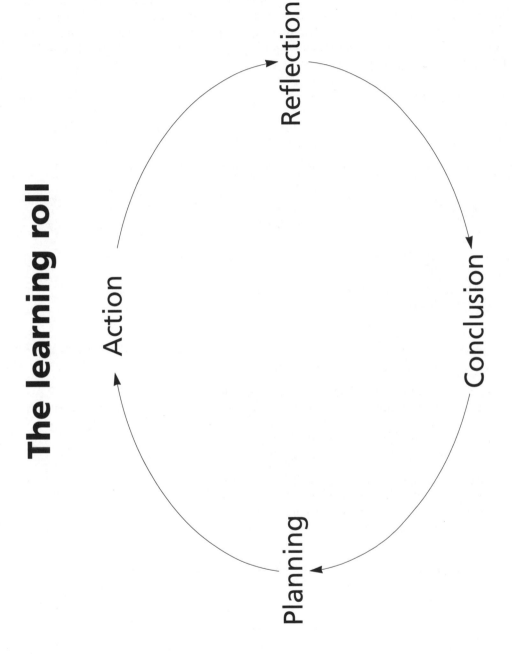

Reproduced from *The Mentoring Manual* by Mike Whittaker and Ann Cartwright, Gower, Aldershot

The Johari Window

The Johari Window provides a useful framework for thinking about those aspects of the self which are known/unknown by the self and by other people. The model, illustrated below, can be used to guide a person towards conscious behaviours aimed to enrich self-development and interpersonal relationships. The OHP transparency copy is opposite.

	KNOWN BY ME ABOUT ME	NOT KNOWN BY ME ABOUT ME
KNOWN BY OTHERS ABOUT ME	OPEN (arena)	BLIND SPOT
NOT KNOWN BY OTHERS ABOUT ME	HIDDEN	UNKNOWN

The 'arena' can be extended in two principal ways:

1   By reducing the 'blind spot'; this can be achieved if:
   ● I ask skilful questions which aim to gather data about others' perceptions of me
   ● other people volunteer information about me
   ● I behave in ways that encourage feedback from others.

2   By reducing the 'hidden' area. This can be achieved if:
   ● I volunteer information about myself (disclosure)
   ● others ask for information about me
   ● I create a climate where others feel comfortable about seeking information from me.

The unknown can be explored by experimenting with new behaviours.

The Johari Window

	KNOWN BY ME ABOUT ME	NOT KNOWN BY ME ABOUT ME
KNOWN BY OTHERS ABOUT ME	**OPEN (arena)**	**BLIND SPOT**
NOT KNOWN BY OTHERS ABOUT ME	**HIDDEN**	**UNKNOWN**

Chapter 2

Mentoring in operation

Introduction

During 1998 and 1999, we talked to people whose organizations already had mentoring in place. We would not claim that these 'studies' cover every situation in which mentoring can flourish. The time spent, however, gave us a snapshot of mentoring in operation and proved to be a series of enjoyable and rewarding experiences which contributed considerably to our own learning.

There should be sufficient here to enable you to review your own existing scheme or to pick out some of the key points to assist you in the process of implementing a completely new one.

We describe a brief history of these schemes with the background to give some indication of why they were originally set up. The areas that we considered were:

- aims
- benefits
- difficulties
- key learning points.

As we move into Chapter 3 we hone in on the most significant aspects of mentoring which we classify under a series of headings.

Sheffield Headteacher Mentoring Scheme

Background

The Sheffield headteacher scheme is essentially a mentoring support mechanism where more experienced headteachers from other schools in the Sheffield area mentor newly appointed heads. It could actually involve a head from a secondary school being mentored by a colleague from a primary school. The scheme was set up in 1992 receiving funding from the Department for Education (DfE). Sheffield, along with other local education authorities, formed the Yorkshire and Humberside Regional Scheme which was responsible for both the first regional training courses and the process of matching mentors to new headteachers.

In 1995, the DfE withdrew the regional funding. Bob McGeachie, who is an ex-head and currently Inspector for the Education Department in Sheffield, drew up the details of the Sheffield mentoring scheme. The scheme continued for a year until the DfE introduced the HEADLAMP scheme for new headteachers. This gave new heads access to spend £2 500 on their own development during the first two years of their headship. The Sheffield Mentoring Scheme has been able to survive because mentoring is a legitimate expenditure under HEADLAMP.

Since its inception 25 heads have received mentoring support which represents a take-up of 80 per cent.

A support group for mentors has been an important part of the scheme although pressure of work and headteachers moving on to other areas have made it difficult to preserve some degree of continuity for this particular support mechanism.

Joan Fallows, Chair of Sheffield Headteacher Mentoring, evaluated the scheme, and in her letter to mentees referred to the fact that 'Sheffield's scheme has continued when most others have collapsed'. Joan's optimism is justified, judging by the positive comments received by the author in talking to a number of heads who were involved in the mentoring process.

Review process

In reviewing the scheme the author was very indebted to the support of Bob McGeachie. Bob, apart from his involvement in setting up the scheme, continues to play an active role in its success. He paved the way for the author to meet Joan Fallows. Joan is both a headteacher and mentor, as well as the chair of the Sheffield scheme. Having met and discussed the scheme with Joan, the author arranged meetings with a cross-section of heads, all of whom had been or still were mentors. One head had herself been mentored and, in turn, became a mentor.

The meetings were informal lasting anything from one to two hours. In every case the reception was warm and friendly which reflected the keen interest in the success of the mentoring process.

Note-taking is always potentially intrusive but the aim was to capture the essential points under some key headings. The following is not intended as a foolproof checklist for the reader but it provides useful information for the review process. The headings are on one sheet of A4 paper with the main title, 'Mentoring Experiences' centred on the page.

- Name
- Date

- Location
- Current involvement
- Training received and reactions
- Different stages of mentoring (mentor's perception of these if appropriate)
- What worked well?
- What was most difficult?
- The *benefits* to you (the mentor)
- The *benefits* to the mentee (the mentor's perception)
- The support mechanism
- Improvements to the mentoring scheme (the mentor's own thoughts)
- What would you (the mentor) do differently or better?

A sample form follows this section (p. 20).

Feedback on the scheme

This feedback is an attempt to summarize the main points arising from the series of meetings. Undoubtedly, there may be omissions and duplications. If, however, the reader is currently struggling to convince others about the merits of mentoring, there should be some useful words here to support your case. It is a balanced view because reference is made to *benefits* on the one hand, and to *difficulties* and possible *improvements* on the other. In beginning with benefits, as in our previous book, *32 Activities on Coaching and Mentoring*, we stress dual benefits to mentor and mentee.

Benefits to the *mentee*

- increased confidence
- support and empathy
- mentor seen as a 'friend' in a potentially isolated environment
- opportunity to let off steam
- helped to confront issues
- shared experiences
- 'She felt unable to do the job; it confirmed she could!'
- 'It got her on her feet'
- re-assurance that his priorities were about right
- helped to establish his key priorities for the following term.

Benefits to the *mentor*

- made me feel good
- clearer vision of what it means to be a head
- put myself in someone else's shoes

- made me use my analytical skills more effectively
- confirmed who are the most important people in the school (the children)
- I feel more comfortable in the job
- I plan more
- improved my communication skills
- I've examined different leadership styles (including my own)
- I realize the skills I've actually got
- brought me tangible benefits, e.g. I'm better organized
- made me feel less isolated
- reminded me that the same things happened to me
- gained fellowship from the support network
- whole process has encouraged exchanges between different schools.

Benefits to the *organization* (schools and education authority)

- better trained headteachers
- mentoring support helps new heads to get to grips with key issues at an early stage in their headship
- helps with professional development
- a group of heads being helped by senior teachers is an integral part of a systematic induction programme.

What have been the major *difficulties*?

The following consist of both the difficulties of being a mentor and those associated with the process itself:

- slow start to our mentoring relationship
- process of building up the relationship
- limited time available
- convincing some that they actually could benefit from having a mentor
- some initial vagueness about the concept of mentoring
- uncomfortable feeling that the mentee may have taken something you've said the wrong way
- danger of thinking you are indispensable to the mentee
- difficulty of ending the mentoring relationship
- accompanying documentation was a bit vague
- mentors move on to other jobs/areas so the pool of potential mentors has declined.

In what way could the scheme be *improved*?

- should be given greater priority by the local authority
- success of the scheme should be publicized more

- secure adequate future funding for the scheme (acknowledging at the same time that this is not an easy task)
- allow more time to do the job properly
- have some more clearly defined guidelines with regard to mentoring and objectives
- improve the matching process
- improve documentation (possibly some form of menu which could be particularly helpful at an early stage in the mentoring relationship)
- introduce some criteria for measuring success
- introduce after two terms in the new job rather than during the first term (not a universally held view)
- include some stress help-lines
- extend the scheme to other levels in the teaching profession.

Key learning points

The Sheffield Headteacher Mentoring Scheme appears to have been well planned and time spent in the careful development of mentors together with an active support group have contributed to the development of new headteachers into crucial and demanding roles. Little can be done about depleting the pool of mentors as some move on to pastures new, other than to select and develop replacements. As part of succession planning a new training programme for mentors will take place in September or October 1999.

The scheme has been in operation for six years, which is a testament to its success. However, there needs to be some fine tuning, such as reviewing the matching process.

Ensuring adequate funding to secure the future and extension of successful schemes like this can be more problematic. To convince others that something like mentoring ultimately can contribute to the more effective running of schools is difficult where key decision-makers may have no intimate knowledge of the subject. Bob McGeachie, however, felt the criticism about the lack of priority given to mentoring by the LEA was a little harsh in that support had been given by the LEA. The training courses referred to earlier have received funding from this source. Other similar mentoring schemes had collapsed and without adequate support the Sheffield scheme could have gone the same way.

The writer believes that the significance of mentoring to support personal development will be increasingly acknowledged. Bob McGeachie, Joan Fallows and the headteachers of Sheffield will continue to prove the benefit of initiatives like this.

REVIEW FORM USED IN RESEARCH

NAME   LOCATION   DATE

CURRENT INVOLVEMENT

TRAINING (details of and reaction to)

OBJECTIVES (statement of and reaction to)

MENTORING EXPERIENCES

DIFFERENT STAGES   BENEFITS TO YOU   BENEFITS TO MENTEE

WHAT WORKED WELL?   WHAT WAS DIFFICULT?

REACTION TO SUPPORT MECHANISM   HOW COULD THE SCHEME
                                       BE IMPROVED?

Reproduced from *The Mentoring Manual* by Mike Whittaker and Ann Cartwright,
Gower, Aldershot

Rotherham Mentoring Programme for Young People

Background

The Rotherham scheme originated in 1995 and received funding from the Single Regeneration Budget. It provides mentoring support to a limited number of young people from selected schools in the Rotherham area. The mentors are neither teachers from the young person's schools nor their parents. Normally in Year 10 at school, the young people have been identified by their teachers as performing below their potential. Their involvement in the programme is in no way obligatory. Since the pilot programme in 1995 more than 100 people have attended a two-day training programme and a majority of these have become mentors. The intention was to establish a high budget, low volume scheme that would build slowly. As part of this strategy, two training programmes are organized each year to gradually augment the pool of mentors.

The Business Education Links team informed employers with whom they were working about the scheme and this provided the source of mentors for the initial training programme. (Earlier, an advertisement seeking mentors failed to draw any response.) Since then word of mouth from existing mentors and the Business Education Link team's own efforts have enabled the pool of mentors to grow.

As part of the matching process mentors and young people complete a questionnaire about personal hobbies and interests. This establishes potential common ground and a meeting is arranged, normally on school premises, to establish the final pairings.

All meetings between mentors and young people take place on school premises in rooms that ensure confidentiality is preserved. They each last for the equivalent of a school period and frequency may vary from eight to 12 meetings per year.

Each school has a nominated teacher to act in a liaison role and this is very much an integral part of the mentoring scheme. Review meetings for those involved in the programme are held regularly to share experiences.

Review process

The writer carried out research on this particular programme as follows:

- discussion with staff from Rotherham Chamber of Commerce Training and Enterprise
- access to several evaluation reports
- discussion with Derek Ainscough, a key player in the setting up of the scheme
- visit to one of the schools actively involved in the scheme, resulting in meetings with teachers, mentors and young people.

In addition to these, the writer became a mentor on the programme and so has experienced at first hand the excellent two-day training programme and the enjoyment of acting as a mentor to a young person.

The successes

Where other similar mentoring schemes may have failed this particular one has enjoyed some success since its inception. Examples of the benefits perceived by those schools taking part are as follows:

- The adult from outside the education system is seen to offer a different perspective to the young person.
- The support is seen as non-threatening.
- The scheme provides the school with the opportunity to raise parents' awareness that there is a potential problem, while offering a possible solution.
- The fact that the school encourages the mentoring relationship shows both parents and pupils that it has recognized a problem and is trying to help.

The following are examples of success stories:

Example A
This boy became involved in the mentoring programme during Years 10 and 11. He had significant personal problems and this resulted in his displaying aggression at school and acting in a confrontational manner. He developed a very good relationship with his mentor and was able to 'chat openly'. As a result, teachers noticed a significant improvement in his behaviour and in his relationship with others.

Example B
This boy lacked self-belief and needed to gain in confidence. He was matched with a mentor who now attends the school every Friday to work with the pupil. The relationship has been very successful.

Example C
This Year 10 girl lacked confidence and the school was very concerned how she would cope with her forthcoming work experience. The scheme has improved her self-confidence and enabled her to perform well on Project Trident (a work experience project).

The writer, in meetings with teachers, mentors and young people was impressed with the way in which some of the young people conducted themselves in what were potentially quite formal situations. On a number of occasions the statement was made, 'You should have seen them a year ago. They simply would have been unable or unwilling to express their feelings in such a confident way.' The writer was left with a lasting impression of young people really believing in themselves.

Difficulties

Most of the comments and experiences are overwhelmingly positive but several difficulties were perceived:

- The scheme seems to be less successful in some schools. This may be dependent upon the level of support within schools. Some schools may not be entirely convinced of the benefits of mentoring.
- Some mentors are no longer able to take part in the scheme. They have re-located or work commitments have made it difficult for them to keep regular appointments.
- Occasionally a mentor has been unable to identify a problem, but the support group suggests that there is no need to be particularly concerned about this.
- Minor administrative difficulties such as relating to the availability of rooms or the school's overlooking an appointment.
- Occasionally a mentor thought some additional background information on the young person could have prevented an inappropriate comment.

Key learning points

At the outset there was a clear intention to establish a high-budget, low-volume mentoring scheme and to build on firm foundations. The scheme has survived and prospered because of an incremental rather than a large-scale approach.

The main expenditure has been on an in-depth and effective training programme for mentors. Each programme has been run in a relaxed and supportive atmosphere, which reflects the subsequent successful relationships between mentors and young people. It might be useful to consider training for mentees as well.

Special attention has been given to the matching process and this has been largely based on similarities in terms of personal interests.

The enthusiasm and support from the mentor liaison teacher in each school are vital ingredients for success of the mentoring scheme within the school.

Given appropriate funding to ensure mentors receive appropriate training, considerable benefits could be derived by extending a similar scheme to younger children.

Large Midlands Engineering Company

Background

The company is a large Midlands based global business that has a strong tradition of training and development especially within the field of engineering. Within the organization most of the professional training undertaken has a formal mentoring process linked to it.

This case study focuses on an informal mentoring process within one of the support services of the organization. At the request of staff in this area, a tool-kit of self-development opportunities was developed to supplement the professional training opportunities that were available to staff. One of these self-development opportunities was mentoring. The programme has now been running for about four years but had not been formally reviewed or evaluated.

Following a discussion with the manager co-ordinating the mentoring option of the self-development tool, it was agreed that Ann Cartwright could conduct a mentee review. The questionnaire – an adapted version of one previously developed by Ann Cartwright – was circulated to 33 participants on the mentoring scheme. (The original questionnaires developed by Ann Cartwright are given on pp. 29–38 although the mentor questionnaire was not eventually used in this review exercise.)

Out of 33 questionnaires issued, 14 were completed and returned. The questions asked focused on two broad areas:

1   about your mentor
2   about the mentoring process.

Open questions were used throughout in order to obtain some qualitative as well as quantitative data.

Analysis of responses

About your mentor

How long have you had a mentor?

At the time of completing the questionnaire (July 1998) the breakdown was as follows:

- 0–6 months   3
- 6–12 months   3
- 1–2 years   0
- 2–3 years   5
- 3–4 years   3

How did you choose your mentor?

- Two people said their mentor was chosen for them.
- Four people took advice and guidance from the mentoring co-ordinator.
- Eight people said that they self-selected their mentor.
- In making their choice the following factors were considered: previous knowledge of the person; respect for the person's integrity, honesty and humour; someone they felt they could get on with; respect for person's experience and knowledge.

Why did you choose your mentor?

There were a range of responses to this question including:

- to provide a sounding board for ideas and provide guidance on issues
- for their experience and knowledge
- I needed some guidance and direction from a more experienced senior manager
- was used in the past to discuss career path, etc.
- was on my selection panel and was genuinely interested in my progress
- role model/best practice in own area
- I needed guidance in work-related situations
- from a recommendation.

How would you describe your mentoring relationship? (e.g. formal, informal, peer, co-mentoring/other)

- Eleven described their mentor relationship as informal. Some used additional words like safe, supportive, relaxed, open, friendly, 'a relationship that's personal to us'.
- Two people described the relationship as both formal and informal.
- One person felt their relationship was formal.

What skills were you looking for in a mentor?

The answers to this question were quite diverse and included the following:

- listening, confidentiality, experience, questioning, challenging, advising
- guidance and knowledge
- proactive as well as a respected member of HR
- to give suggestions, encouragement, guidance, even a shoulder to cry on!
- listening, questioning, ability to 'put their self in my shoes', knowledge of the bigger picture, knowledge of people
- good listener, shows empathy, offering advice and support
- listening, coaching, able to offer advice
- understands me and could be honest in a constructive way
- company knowledge and experience, someone who is respected and who respects me, open and approachable
- able to offer guidance, support and advice on how I could best develop myself
- experienced in HR issues/company issues, coaching and counselling
- informal approach but professional and informative advice
- guidance, contacts, authority, experience
- good listener and adviser, honest and friendly.

What skills does your mentor have?

All 14 people stated that their mentor did have the skills they said they were looking for.

About your mentoring process (from your experience of the mentoring process)

What are the main skills needed by a mentor?

- main skill was *listening*
- questioning and challenging
- coaching and counselling
- able to give advice
- openness, trust and confidentiality
- knowledge and understanding of the business was also very important for the people in the survey.

What are the key features of a successful mentoring relationship?

- being able to open up discussions at all levels
- meeting *your* needs
- able to get on at a personal level, trust and confidence within the relationship, the relationship needs to be continual, with meetings at regular intervals
- understanding and respect for one another's view
- trust and honesty along with confidentiality
- flexibility, informality
- good two-way communication and feedback between mentor and mentee
- the mentor should be from outside your organization; easily approached; regular contact; good advice
- open/honesty; trusting each other; give and take; accepting/respecting each other's views; confidentiality
- open accepting atmosphere and genuine interest; prepared to share experiences – this is not a counselling relationship; appropriate use of empathy and humour
- trust, liking each other, can share a joke, i.e. relax
- honesty, reliability, friendship
- trust; open and honest discussions; realistic advice.

How would you sell the benefits of mentoring to others?

- by presentation, leaflet, video – many other ways of PR
- by emphasizing the need and advantage to talk to someone who's independent
- someone with whom ideas can be tested and to tap into someone else's network
- that if nothing else it is a good, confidential (if you choose) sounding board
- objective and honest feedback, long-term relationship
- useful to have someone to talk to who is away from the everyday working environment
- aid to personal development, talking in confidence
- explain how it can help your career by guidance on decisions, promotions, etc.
- reflect on my own experience especially where it's been of value

- I'd tell them about the scheme or hand out the brochure or refer to Mr B. I mention the mentoring scheme when I have training review meetings with managers
- an opportunity to benefit from someone's experience. Knowing someone else is interested and to whom you can speak honestly without endangering your career
- it is an independent, confidential relationship you have with a fellow human resources colleague
- mentoring gives you the opportunity to discuss career opportunities with someone outside of your normal job remit in an honest but confidential way
- sounding board for ideas in a safe environment, 'Get issues off your chest'. Career advice. Build up a network of contact or point you to someone who could help.

What training/guidance, if any, do you feel people should have before they enter into a mentoring relationship?

- explanation of what the scheme should be used for
- go through the mentoring process with someone experienced on the process
- what to expect of the mentor would be helpful and to talk to someone who has had or has the same mentor
- depends on relationship, i.e. mentors may need engineering qualifications, for instance, human resources mentor may require training in personal skills (but not mine)
- not too much, the relationship should be automatic or else you have chosen the wrong mentor
- mentors should have experience from being a mentee to understand how the relationship should work. They should also experience some formal training
- counselling skills really
- let them know the benefits
- counselling skills; mentoring training
- understand the role and responsibilities of a mentor and have the ability to maintain the commitment and integrity required
- when to get in touch with mentor. Should we meet regularly?
- I believe both parties have to understand the role so one knows whether they can/are prepared to deliver and the other knows what to expect
- guidance through awareness sessions. Something needs to be in place for the scheme to be successful
- workshop based guidance – all mentors trained together so they can share information and all mentees together for the same reason.

Conclusions

The mentoring scheme has now been running for about four years and seems to be running successfully. Almost all of the respondents think that they have benefited from the scheme.

Based on some of the responses from the last question it may be advisable to revisit the training/briefing process especially for the mentees

The respondents were all mentees and it is clear from their responses that they all found the process helpful. In order to carry out a more comprehensive review of the process it would be necessary to gather views from the mentors as well.

Recommendations to the company

In order to obtain a balanced view of the mentoring scheme it is recommended that a similar review be carried out on the mentors. This will help to identify what additional support and training they may need as well as confirming the range and level of personal development they have acquired through the mentoring process.

Final comments

At the time of writing, although the company had accepted the principle of using a similar questionnaire to review the mentors, they had not carried out the review. The forms used on this review example are included in the next few pages (pp. 29–38).

MENTOR'S REVIEW QUESTIONNAIRE

Name:

Contact address:

Telephone:

About you as a mentor

How long have you been a mentor?

How many people do you mentor and/or have you mentored?

Why did you choose to become a mentor?

How would you describe your mentoring relationship(s)? (e.g. formal /informal/peer/co-mentoring/other)

What training did you receive before you started mentoring?

How helpful was this training?

On reflection, what additional training or support would you have liked?

What benefits do you feel you have gained from this mentoring relationship?

Could you have gained these benefits from any other type of training or development? If yes, please describe.

At the start of this mentoring relationship did you agree any terms of reference or ground rules?

What review processes if any did you build into this relationship?

How effective were these processes?

What if anything would you like to change about this mentoring relationship?

What, if anything, is likely to end this mentoring relationship?

About the mentoring process

From your experience of the mentoring process:

What are the main skills needed by a mentor?

What are the key features of a successful mentoring relationship?

How would you sell the benefits of mentoring to others?

What training/guidance if any do you feel people should have before they enter into a mentoring relationship?

What ongoing support systems do you think mentors should have, if any?

Are you willing for this information to be written up as a case study?

Thank you for taking the time to complete this questionnaire.

Please return completed questionnaire to:

MENTEE'S REVIEW QUESTIONNAIRE

Name:

Contact address:

Telephone:

About your mentor

How long have you had a mentor?

How did you choose your mentor?

Why did you choose your mentor?

Reproduced from *The Mentoring Manual* by Mike Whittaker and Ann Cartwright, Gower, Aldershot

How would you describe your mentoring relationship? (e.g. formal /informal/peer/co-mentoring/other)

What skills were you looking for in a mentor?

What skills does your mentor have?

What benefits do you feel you have gained from this mentoring relationship?

Could you have gained these benefits from any other type of training or development? If yes, please describe.

At the start of this mentoring relationship did you agree any terms of reference or ground rules?

What review processes if any did you build into this relationship?

How effective were these processes?

What if anything would you like to change about this mentoring relationship?

What, if anything, is likely to end this mentoring relationship?

About the mentoring process

From your experience of the mentoring process:

What are the main skills needed by a mentor?

What are the key features of a successful mentoring relationship?

How would you sell the benefits of mentoring to others?

What training/guidance if any do you feel people should have before they enter into a mentoring relationship?

Are you willing for this information to be written up as a case study?

Thank you for taking the time to complete this questionnaire.

Please return completed questionnaire to:

Wakefield and Pontefract GP Mentoring Scheme

Background

Some interest has been shown in the last five years in providing mentoring support for general practitioners (GPs) in various regions of the UK, e.g. South Thames, East Anglia and Yorkshire. This particular scheme is located in the Wakefield and Pontefract area and was initiated in 1996. It was developed through a collaboration between Wakefield and Pontefract GP Continuing Medical Education tutors, Dr Mark Napper (Wakefield) and Dr Richard Sloan (Pontefract), a senior consultant from the training organization ITS, Derek Powell, and the Director of Postgraduate General Practice Education for the Yorkshire Deanery, Dr Jamie Bahrami. Financial support was provided by the Yorkshire Deanery. Information about the proposed scheme was sent to all GPs in the Wakefield and Pontefract area. Seventeen people were initially recruited to the programme.

The aims of the scheme were described as:

- to facilitate the personal and professional development of general practitioners
- to help general practitioners identify and meet their continuing medical educational needs
- to encourage general practitioners to reflect upon their work
- to provide support for general practitioners.

All the GPs completed the intensive development programme that considered the role of mentoring, helped to develop mentoring skills and looked at the practicalities of implementation. Use was made of CCTV in the process of developing skills.

After the development programme was completed details of the scheme itself and biographical notes of each mentor were sent to all GPs in the area. The matching process began by each respondent selecting the five potential mentors with whom they would like to work in ascending order. The 'one to one' final selection was then confirmed by the mentoring facilitator. Mentors also work in 'co-mentoring' pairs which helps to develop their skills. Additional peer support is available as a result of regular meetings. These enable mentors to share learning and experiences and provide a useful source of new ideas.

Some feedback from the mentoring sessions themselves suggests that after initial focus on personal issues the tendency was to move on to professional and development matters.

Review process

Mark Napper and Derek Powell presented a session at the 4th European Mentoring Conference in London in November 1997. The writer who subsequently arranged meetings with Mark and Derek in March and October 1998 also attended this. This section in the book is therefore based on the separate discussions and the London presentation.

The successes

- increased level of confidence
- 'rescued from a major disaster'
- enabled mentees to work on individual education plans
- the motivation and enthusiasm of mentors
- enabled mentees to 'move on'.

The difficulties

There are two aspects to consider here. One is the Wakefield and Pontefract scheme itself; the other, and the one now to be discussed, concerns circumstances surrounding the medical profession itself. The process of becoming a GP involves a formal education system based on acquiring factual information through traditional teaching methods. Mentoring involves an approach that may not be within the immediate experience of either or both mentor and mentee. For example, someone considering the option of being a mentee might ask, 'How is this approach going to help me develop my career?' Alternatively, they might say, 'Yes, I may need help, but I'm supposed to be this infallible GP who helps others. It feels uncomfortable to me to admit any form of weakness.' There is also the question of confidentiality. If a GP is mentoring a colleague who is suffering extreme mental pressure for example, what might be the consequences for his patients? What does the mentor do in terms of disclosure to others? The General Medical Council has made it clear that it is a doctor's ethical responsibility to act where they believe a colleague's conduct, performance or health is a threat to patients.

The importance of maintaining confidentiality is critical to the success of all mentoring schemes. Mentoring within the medical profession has additional ethical considerations. In the case of the Wakefield and Pontefract scheme at the early contracting stage mentees had the option to clarify the areas to be covered in the relationship. In other words, certain aspects could be declared out of bounds, but this could, of course, affect the depth of the mentoring relationship. Potentially, 'A mentoring partnership could become one that avoids honestly dealing with some of the issues it reveals, becoming instead one that is collusive' (a quote from Mark Napper and Derek Powell's London presentation).

This in no way denigrates the success of the Wakefield and Pontefract scheme, but it shows how difficult it could be to implement mentoring within the medical profession because of cultural and ethical considerations.

Some of the difficulties experienced with this particular scheme were as follows:

- selling the concept of mentoring to GPs
- comparatively low take-up from quite a high investment in time and financial resources
- new GPs in the main have not taken up the option to receive mentoring support
- momentum of the scheme will be lost if mentors who have gone through the development programme are not able to put the skills into practice
- some mentors found some difficulty either at the start or end of the relationship or both.

Key learning points

Mark Napper pointed out that the scheme has enjoyed some success but an important consideration for him is maintaining momentum. Given the benefit of hindsight key considerations would be:

- To be slightly less ambitious at the start of the scheme and recruit fewer mentors.
- To think more about the most effective means of promoting the scheme, which would place more emphasis on gaining interest through personal contact rather than a brochure.
- To spend more time on skills development.

Overall the scheme seems to have enjoyed some success, particularly given the difficult circumstances and pressures experienced in the medical profession.

Women's Co-mentoring Scheme – East Midlands

Background

This case study outlines the problems and difficulties associated with trying to establish a mentoring scheme for women managers working within the voluntary sector in an East Midlands city.

The idea for the scheme was identified after a number of discussions with women managers working in a variety of voluntary sector organizations across the city. In total, about 20 women had individually and collectively identified that they worked in a degree of isolation either as lone workers or as the most senior worker in their respective organizations. The shared difficulties they experienced included not having access to someone they could confide in and discuss work-related issues and problems. All of the women reported to a management committee consisting of voluntary trustees or board members. Many of the women felt that despite being helpful and supportive, confiding in individual members of the management committee was inappropriate because they were the equivalent of a line manager. As a result the women often felt unsupported and isolated within their roles and were looking for some way of resolving the situation.

Originally, it was suggested that a network of *peer supervision* be established in an attempt to provide some peer support. This was later defined as a co-mentoring network. The aim of the co-mentoring network was to:

● establish a database of women who wanted this type of mutual support
● identify what each person wanted from the process and what they thought they were able to give to the process
● match the partners and provide training and support to assist them to establish effective relationships
● provide ongoing guidance and support to each partnership as requested and required.

To begin with, the co-mentoring network was co-ordinated by the management advisor based at the local Council for Voluntary Services (CVS) and a small number of partnerships were established. (Ann Cartwright was involved in one of these partnerships and a summary of this relationship is included on the opposite page.) However, very little was done to support and guide these partnerships so many of them did not succeed. In addition, when the management advisor left the CVS, there was no-one to act as co-ordinator and as a result the network effectively died.

The process was re-launched when a new management advisor was appointed by the CVS. This time it was agreed that more training was needed to explain the process, identify the key skills required, establish and support the partnerships. A series of evening workshops were organized to do this. However, for a number of reasons including pressures of work, many of the women were unable to attend the workshops or give the process the degree of commitment it needed. Providing the training and support was also becoming problematical as it relied on Ann Cartwright volunteering her time and expertise because there was no funding to pay for the training. When the second management advisor left the CVS, once again the network fell into decline.

A third and final attempt was made to revive the network, but this was short-lived because no one was able to devote the time to co-ordinate it and apply for funding to make it work.

Lessons

1   Trying to organize this type of network takes time and commitment and, more importantly, needs funding. It is very difficult to try to do this type of activity on a purely voluntary basis.
2   The levels of commitment needed to sustain personal development of this nature on top of a working day are often greater than people are able to give. The network would have been more successful if time could have been found within the working day to attend. Sadly most people were not able to give time in the day.

3   Managers, especially voluntary sector managers, are not able to justify to their employers or funders that time spent on their development is time that benefits both them and their organization in the medium and long term. This attitude has to change if we want to develop successful managers in the future.

Ann Cartwright's partnership experience

My co-mentor and I met on average once a month for about one-hour each taking about 30 minutes to raise and discuss any issues or areas of concerns that we had experienced since our last meeting. We both found the sessions useful the last time we met. The relationship was temporarily on hold due to illness.

Key benefits we both gained from the process include:

● Being able to discuss and raise issues of concern in an environment that was safe with a person who was detached from the situation and who was able to understand the issues.
● Having someone to question and challenge one's thinking in a non-threatening way.
● Being able to consider and think through options and possible solutions, take actions and then come back and talk over the impact and outcomes of these actions.
● Understanding and improving the way we did things.

Co-mentoring Scheme – East Midlands

Background

This case study focuses on recent attempts to introduce a co-mentoring scheme for chief executives and senior managers within an East Midlands city. Following some initial discussion with the local Training and Enterprise Council (TEC), they agreed to fund some work to test the potential interest among local chief executives and senior managers in co-mentoring.

What is co-mentoring?

● The aim of co-mentoring is to provide participants with a cost-effective process of self-managed development that both meets their needs and fits into their time constraints.

- Co-mentoring is an *equal* relationship between two people who value and respect each other and who believe that each has something to offer the other. By sharing their experiences, issues and concerns within an equal and trusting environment, each person can continue to develop and grow and so maximize their respective potential.

- Co-mentoring is *not* about two people having a conversation. It is a two-way process that gives each person an agreed period of 'unconditional time and space' to talk through issues, ideas and situations that are unique to them. For example, 30 minutes of unconditional time and space per person. Most of us are not used to giving or receiving unconditional time and space, so the process will require some practice.

- Co-mentoring is an opportunity to use someone as a 'sounding board' for new ideas and initiatives. It also provides an opportunity for constructive reflection with someone who will be open and honest.

- Co-mentoring is an effective self-development tool for busy people.

How does co-mentoring work?

- Each partner agrees to how much time is available for the session.

- The 'listening' partner may check understanding or seek clarification of a point but otherwise must *not* interrupt the 'speaking' partner during the agreed period of unconditional time and space. The 'listening' partner should *not* make any value judgements or insist that the 'speaking' partner justify their actions.

- At the end of the agreed period of unconditional time and space, the 'listening' partner should reflect back to the 'speaking' partner what was said, question and challenge any issues, give feedback on any issues and so on. Each partner can agree beforehand any issues or points that they would like the 'listening' partner to focus on, if appropriate.

- Partners should then swap roles and repeat the process.

- The timings and frequency of meetings can be agreed between the partners to fit in with their needs and time constraints.

How was the initiative developed?

The local TEC regularly ran breakfast briefing sessions for chief executives on a wide variety of topics and as a result they had quite a large database of chief executives across the local area. It was agreed that, using this database, a briefing sheet on co-mentoring would be sent out along with an invitation to attend an introductory workshop. The workshop was designed to provide chief executives and senior managers with:

- an overview of the concepts and principles of co-mentoring
- an opportunity to explore how the process could be of benefit to them
- an opportunity to be 'matched' to a co-mentoring partner.

The TEC was also willing to fund some ongoing support and development identified by the participants.

The initial response to this initiative was very encouraging. Out of a circulation of about 100 people, about 25 people said that they would attend the introductory workshop, with another 25 people expressing an interest in the initiative who were not able to attend the introductory session.

About 20 people attended the introductory workshop. At the end of the workshop most people were agreed that they would like to give co-mentoring a try and that the simplest way to find a potential partner was to adopt a 'blind date' approach. In order to facilitate this, participants agreed that interested people would complete and return a profile sheet (see pp. 46–48). Once returned, the sheets were randomly matched and copies were sent to perspective partners to arrange initial meetings.

At the time of writing this book, five partnerships (i.e. 10 people) have been established and each of these partnerships has met at least once. The TEC have agreed to fund a further review meeting:

- to check on the progress of the co-mentoring partnerships
- to identify any additional support needs that the partnerships might have
- to explore if and how the benefits of co-mentoring should be publicized.

Conclusions

This is a new and ongoing development that has not yet demonstrated many clear and tangible outcomes. However, it is clear from follow-up conversations with the co-mentoring partners that they are all keen to give the process a serious try.

CO-MENTOR PARTNER PROFILE SHEET

Name:

Job title:

Organization:

Address:

Telephone: Fax:
E-mail:

Number of years in present position:

I would use the following five adjectives or phrases to describe myself:

1

2

3

4

5

Reproduced from *The Mentoring Manual* by Mike Whittaker and Ann Cartwright,
Gower, Aldershot

I would use the following five adjectives or phrases to describe the type of co-mentor I would like to work with:

1

2

3

4

5

I have identified that my two key development needs are:

1

2

The skills, experiences and behaviours I believe I can give to a co-mentor partnership are:

The skills, experiences and behaviours I am looking for from a co-mentoring partnership are:

I would like to be matched to a co-mentoring partner.   Yes/No

I would like to find my own co-mentoring partner.   Yes/No

I am happy that this information is shared with my potential co-mentoring partner.   Yes/No

I agree to make contact with my potential co-mentoring partner within 10 days of receiving their details.   Yes/No

Summary of key learning points

This is an attempt to extract the key learning points from our studies. While some of these may be expressed in negative terms, we think the difficulties and problems provide real learning opportunities.

Your mentoring scheme may be somewhat different from the examples quoted but take from this section anything you feel will help, either prior to implementation or as part of a review. In Chapter 3, we break mentoring down into the key elements.

Sheffield Headteacher Mentoring Scheme

- ensure you have adequate funding
- have clearly defined guidelines on both the purpose and process
- broadcast mentoring successes.

Rotherham Mentoring Programme for Young People

- a high-budget, low-volume approach worked well; build your scheme on firm foundations
- much of the success depends on the interest and support of each school's mentor liaison teacher
- a series of effective training programmes contributed to the success of the scheme.

Large Midlands Engineering Company

- more time should be spent on the clarification of objectives and the role of mentors
- ensure all the mentors are trained together; the same applies to mentees
- to gain commitment to mentoring tell mentees beforehand about the potential benefits that accrue from it.

Wakefield and Pontefract GP Mentoring Scheme

- avoid being over-ambitious at the start of a scheme
- a scheme will lose momentum if mentors, after having been trained, are not able to put their skills into practice
- it is sometimes easier to sell the concept of mentoring and to gain potential mentors by personal contacts, rather than relying on formal means such as brochures.

Women's Co-mentoring Scheme – East Midlands

- ran into some difficulties because no one person had the time to take on the co-ordinating role
- trying to organize a network like this took time and commitment and needed some form of funding, which all proved very difficult to achieve on a voluntary basis

- time needs to be spent in convincing others of the benefits of mentoring.

Co-mentoring Scheme – East Midlands

This is a recently established scheme and the early indications are as follows:

- chief executives and senior managers do not always perceive themselves to be in control of their own time and learning. Although there was a considerable interest in the concept, very few actually returned the profile sheet. This may have been due to a lack of time or if they may have been afraid of being set up with a co-mentoring partner on a 'blind date'.

- feedback from the few people who did return the profiles and who were matched on 'blind dates' indicated that they found the initial meetings very productive and were intending to set up more meetings.

Chapter 3

Practical considerations

Introduction

We would like to think there will be something in this chapter for you whatever your involvement is in mentoring. So, you could be a mentee, mentor, facilitator or the decision-maker with the power/influence to say 'Yes' or 'No' to mentoring. It is probably going to be of most practical use to the person who has the responsibility for setting up, administrating and reviewing a mentoring scheme. We use the word 'facilitator' but in the organization your job title could be training manager, human resources manager, or administrator.

There are three sections to this chapter:

I   The 11 key areas (page 52)
II   Suggestions for effective mentoring – a summary of the 11 key areas (page 131)
III The mentoring relationship (page 135).

In Section I the 11 key areas are as follows:

1   Setting objectives
2   Planning the introduction of a programme
3   Key roles in mentoring
4   Influencing strategy
5   Mentoring and culture
6   The matching process
7   Training
8   Administration
9   Setting up support networks
10   Monitoring and evaluation
11   What can go wrong?

Section II is a summary of essential features of effective mentoring.

Section III focuses on individual mentoring relationships but in the form of an outsider looking on. Because confidentiality and discretion are essential ingredients of effective mentoring this focus may appear to be problematical. In practice, it means the facilitator seeks feedback on process from mentees and mentors and not hard data that emerges from the relationships. Both parties must in any case be in full agreement before anything is discussed with a third party. The whole purpose of involving a third party is to learn as much as possible about effective mentoring relationships; this learning can be then passed on to others.

I   The 11 key areas

1   Setting objectives

Introduction

At frequent intervals in mentoring someone is bound to ask, 'Why are we involved in mentoring' and 'Where are we going?' These questions could be appropriate in a number of contexts and the following are three examples:

i   What is the overall purpose of mentoring in our organization?
ii   In our specific mentor/mentee relationship, what are the sort of things we are trying to achieve?
iii What are the main objectives for this particular mentoring training event that I am attending/running?

We will cover examples (ii) and (iii) elsewhere in the book (see Key Areas 3 (page 71) and 7 (page 98)), so at this stage we are making the assumption that you are either considering the main purpose behind your setting up a mentoring scheme or taking time out to review what you already do.

General purpose or specific objectives?

At the risk of using a well-worn expression, we could talk about 'fit for purpose'. So you may decide to choose something which is simply a brief statement about the overall aim:

● help with personal development
● help with personal issues
● guidance into new roles
● support professional development
● support for 'under-achievers'

- a sounding board for ideas and issues, e.g. co-mentoring
- encourage equality, e.g. for ethnic minorities, disabled people or women aiming for senior management positions in traditionally white, male-dominated and/or able-bodied cultures
- support to other development/change programmes.

You may well wish to use a simple statement as a starting point and then move to something with the detail of the GP mentoring scheme described in Chapter 2 (pp. 39–41):

> The scheme aims:
>
> - To facilitate the personal and professional development of general practitioners.
> - To help general practitioners identify and meet their continuing medical educational needs.
> - To encourage GPs to reflect upon their work.
> - To provide support for GPs.

The following aims are included in a scheme where trainee teachers are mentors to Year 11 pupils:

> The aims are to develop in pupils:
>
> - positive attitudes towards long-term education and opportunities post 16
> - decision-making skills for the setting of short, medium and long term goals
> - self-confidence.

You may wish to move from the general aims to the more specific. You could consider the SMART acronym. There are a number of variations on this but this is one version:

S   Specific
M   Measurable
A   Achievable
R   Realistic
T   Time-bound

There may appear to be some potential conflict between the 'soft' and supportive nature of mentoring and the more specific objectives behind something like SMART. If it helps you to focus on what you hope mentoring will achieve, why not use it? Remember, you may have somebody saying to you, 'I'm not sure what this mentoring is all about. I need you to persuade me why we should seriously consider using it here.'

On the other hand, the writer feels you need to avoid something such as: 'Within two years the mentoring scheme will enable 95 per cent of our students to achieve GCSE Grade 1 in eight subjects.'

Agreeing and communicating objectives

It will be advisable to test your own initial thoughts on the main purpose behind mentoring with others in the organization. If the initiative is likely to receive active support from your chief executive it makes sense to encourage this support. Life is not, however, always as simple as that and it may be a case of getting something in place on a small scale, getting reactions from those most likely to benefit from mentoring or those most receptive to such an initiative.

If your task is to get mentoring in place, reactions from others will be invaluable. You may need to modify your first thoughts. Perhaps your enthusiasm is getting the better of you and you are expecting too much from it. Keep things simple. This makes it easier to communicate the main aims of the scheme to both mentors and mentees.

Reviewing objectives

Having established the main purpose of the scheme and communicated this to those involved (not forgetting to include line managers) there needs to be some form of review:

1   Are the objectives still valid?
2   Do they need to be redefined?
3   Is it appropriate to extend the scheme to others?
4   If there are difficulties in meeting the initial objectives what changes need to be made?

The review of objectives could involve discussion with mentors and mentees, line managers, and any other support mechanism in place.

Summary

1   Think of the main purpose of mentoring in your organization.
2   Obtain reactions from others.
3   Get final agreement on objectives and write these into the summary of the scheme.
4   Ensure the objectives are communicated to those involved.
5   Review objectives periodically and amend if necessary.
6   Extend the scope of scheme if appropriate.

On pages 55–57 is a form, which will enable you to follow the process of establishing mentoring objectives.

ESTABLISHING MENTORING OBJECTIVES

What is the target group?	Job titles	Number

Source of mentors	Job titles	Number

Initial thoughts on the main purpose of mentoring

Who should I consult on mentoring?

Summary of this discussion

Revised mentoring objectives

Benefits of mentoring to:

1   Mentee

2   Mentor

3   Organization

Mentoring objectives review   Date

Reproduced from *The Mentoring Manual* by Mike Whittaker and Ann Cartwright,   *57*
Gower, Aldershot

2   Planning the introduction of a programme

Who do you need to involve?

If you are planning to introduce a mentoring programme into your organization you need to give careful consideration to the key people you will need to involve if it is to become a success. These people will differ from one organization to another, but it is possible to identify some generic roles.

Programme champion or sponsor

The sponsor is likely to be a senior manager in the organization such as:

- the managing director or chief executive
- the head of human resource development
- an operational manager/director with a keen interest in the development of people and who has the respect and 'ear' of other senior managers.

You may need to outline and explain to this person, the concepts of mentoring and the benefits that mentoring can bring to individuals, both mentors and mentees as well as the organization. This could be done either by arranging a meeting or by preparing a report. You will know from your knowledge of the organization which approach will work the best. Either way, you may want to stress some of the following features of mentoring as a development tool:

- Mentoring is an effective, low-cost development option compared to other types of development such as short courses or day release.
- Mentoring provides a development opportunity for both the mentor and the mentee.
- Mentoring can be a useful way of developing cross-departmental working and co-operation by arranging that mentees be matched with mentors from different departments.
- Mentoring can help to bring about change and continuous improvement within the organization because the process actively encourages the ongoing reflection of behaviours and actions as well as identifying options for doing things differently or better next time around.
- Mentoring can be used to improve the performance of individuals through the use of action plans agreed at the end of each session and reviewed at the following session.
- Mentoring is an excellent way of demonstrating an organization's commitment to initiatives like the 'Investors in People' standard.

There may well be other 'hooks' that you are aware of within your organization that can be used to persuade this key person to support you in the introduction of a mentoring programme. At this point, you may also need to identify what ongoing support you would require from this key person to ensure the long-term success of the programme and what role you expect the key person to take in selling the idea to other managers.

You may like to suggest that this key person take on the role of your mentor throughout the introduction of the programme.

Potential participants both mentors and mentees

Once the idea of introducing a mentoring programme has been given approval, you will need to turn your attention more fully to the likely participants in such a scheme. You will need to identify who in the organization would be willing and able to become mentors and who would want to become mentees.

There are numerous ways of doing this and you will know the option that would best suit your organization. However, listed below are some general ideas and approaches that you might want to try.

Recruiting mentors

- Write to all the managers in your organization explaining briefly what the mentoring programme is about and invite them to attend an introductory workshop so you can explain in more detail the concepts process and time commitments involved in becoming a mentor. You will find some outlines for mentoring workshops later in this book (pp. 98–100 and pp. 173–183).

- Consider each of the managers within the organization and identify which of them would make good mentors. Either speak to them individually or invite them to an introductory workshop.

- If your organization has a staff newsletter, write an article on mentoring and invite interested people to get in touch with you.

- If your organization runs an in-house training and development programme arrange for a mentoring workshop to be included in the programme.

Recruiting mentees

- If your organization has a staff newsletter write an article on mentoring and invite interested people to get in touch with you.

- If your organization runs an in-house training and development programme arrange for a mentoring workshop to be included in the programme.

- Ask managers in the organization to identify which of their staff would benefit from the mentoring programme.

- Include the concept of mentoring within the induction process and encourage all new members of staff to sign up as mentees.

- In certain professional disciplines such as engineering, the process of mentoring is a mandatory part of the training process. In this instance the mentoring process tends to focus purely on technical/professional aspects and may not cover any personal development. If your organization operates in this environment you may need to sell the personal development aspects and benefits of your mentoring scheme in a different way.

The scope of mentoring

Once you have sold the concepts and benefits of mentoring to key people within the organization and identified some potential mentor and mentees, you will need to give some thought to the scope of the mentoring programme that you want to introduce within the organization. For example:

- Do you see it as part of a range of training and development tools that is made available to all staff or will it only be available to certain groups of staff?
- Will participation on the scheme always remain voluntary or do you envisage that once a person has signed up to the mentoring process they must continue with it at all costs?
- How will mentors and mentees be matched?
- How will their progress be monitored?
- What guidelines will you provide to participants about the mentoring process?
- What grievance or arbitration processes will there be in the scheme in case any disagreements arise between the mentor and mentee?
- Under what circumstances will you allow a mentee to change mentors and vice versa?
- What happens when a mentee outgrows their mentor?
- How does the mentoring process fit into other training and development strategies with the organization?
- What other support mechanisms will the programme include, for example: skills development workshops for mentors; support sessions for mentors and mentees to discuss and share their common experiences and difficulties with the process; training prior to the start of the programme?
- Who will act as programme facilitator or broker?
- How will the programme be monitored and reviewed and how often?
- How will success be measured?

The answer to most of these questions will be determined by the specific needs of your organization. But we give you examples of the sort of issues you might need to address. For example, this manual includes:

- An example of a mentoring profile sheet that you may find useful.

- Some options for matching mentors and mentees for you to consider.
- Some examples about what different types of workshops you could and should include and has made reference to potential sources of learning materials you could use.
- An example of guidance notes that could be given to participants.
- Some questionnaires that could be used by both mentors and mentees to review your scheme.
- Some case studies from other organizations that you might find useful examples of things to duplicate and/or things to avoid.

Anticipating how it might develop?

Depending on the response you get from people within your organization, your mentoring programme could either sink like a lead weight or fly like a kite. Either way you need to give some thought to how your programme is likely to develop and how you can effectively manage that process.

Assuming the scheme takes off and you have generated a huge amount of interest in the scheme, how will this be managed within the organization and who will take responsibility for co-ordinating the process? A successful scheme will take quite a lot of organizing. For example, someone will need to co-ordinate and keep records about:

- *The mentors* – who they are, which area or department they are from, who they are mentoring and where the mentee is from, when the mentoring started and ended, what additional training and/or support they have asked for.
- *The mentees* – who they are, which area or department they are from, who is acting as their mentor and where the mentor is from, when the mentoring started and ended, any problems or difficulties with the partnership, what additional training and/or support they have asked for.
- *The reviews* – how often will they happen, who will need the information and how often, how will success be measured, what methods will be used to carry out the review, e.g. questionnaires, personal interviews, how will changes to the process be introduced and communicated, how will success be celebrated?

All of the above could be very time-consuming and, depending on the size of the organization, could become a full-time job in itself. If that were the case, there are obvious resource implications that need to be considered. These would need to be balanced against the cost benefits to the organization.

In some cases, too much demand too soon could work against the success of the scheme. If the initial stages of mentoring are not managed and co-ordinated effectively the scheme could sink like a lead weight before it has had a chance to prove itself. An example of this can be seen in the case study of the Women's Co-mentoring Scheme (pp. 41–43). One of the key reasons this scheme failed was that there was no one with the time to take on the task of co-ordinating it.

It may be better to try to manage the growth of the scheme more slowly by setting up a pilot project.

The benefits of a pilot project approach

- A pilot project could be set up in one department or section or by restricting the scheme to one particular discipline.
- Establishing a pilot scheme could also be a useful way of 'selling' the benefits to any sceptical managers you might have in the organization.
- Within the pilot programme you will be able to restrict the number of potential participants and as a result reduce the size of the co-ordinating task.
- Participants from the pilot scheme could be used to 'sell' the scheme and its benefits to others.
- Mentees from the pilot scheme could become mentors for new participants if appropriate.
- A pilot scheme would enable you to gather evidence about the specific individual and organizational benefits that can be gained from the mentoring process. This evidence can then be used to make a stronger case for expanding the scheme and for dedicating additional resources to it.

Considerations on both informal and formal approaches

As stated earlier, some disciplines and professions include a formal and mandatory mentoring process as part of their learning programme. There are some lessons that you can learn from this approach and some issues that you might want to consider before trying to introduce your own scheme. Listed below are a few comments and ideas that you might like to consider.

The concept and thinking behind having formal and mandatory mentoring as part of the professional development process has a number of benefits and disadvantages. For example:

- Benefits include:
  - Matching a trainee professional with an experienced professional gives the trainee access to a level and range of practical experiences, skills and knowledge that would be difficult to replicate in a classroom setting or through written material alone.
  - It mirrors all the good points of the old craft apprenticeship process, i.e. young apprentice learning from the experienced trades-person.
- Disadvantages include:
  - The trainee is often taught all the bad habits of the mentor along with the positive ones.
  - The benefits of the mentoring process is not always systematically

monitored and there is often no process for resolving any grievances between the mentor and mentee.

– The formal and mandatory nature of the process often results in both the mentor and the mentee simply 'going through the motion' without really learning from the process.

We often have a tendency to resist or rebel against anything that is made compulsory or mandatory. Any task, action or activity seems to become a chore rather than a pleasure or something we do willingly when we feel we are being forced into it. 'I want to do something' has a different feel to it than 'I have to do something'. The first suggests a sense of choice and desire, the latter a sense of compulsion and potential punishment if it's not done.

Introducing a formal and mandatory mentoring scheme in your organization could have the negative effect just mentioned. You will need to consider if and how you can include a sense of choice within the mentoring process. Some ways of including choice are by:

● ensuring that the process is regularly reviewed and revised to check that both the mentor and the mentee are gaining some benefits from the process.

● including a grievance and/or arbitration process within the scheme that both mentors and mentees can use to raise any problems or difficulties that they are unable to resolve themselves.

● establishing separate support systems and meetings for mentors and mentees to enable them to discuss and share experiences and explore ways of resolving problems and difficulties without having to refer them to the grievance or arbitration process.

● allowing participants to terminate a mentoring relationship when either or both people feel it is right for them.

In some instances the mentoring process happens in an informal way, sometimes planned but often not. You may be able to identify from your own experiences an example of informal mentoring. It could have been a relative, teacher or family friend who was always on hand to offer you advice or guidance. Perhaps there is someone from your working life that acted as your informal mentor. Maybe you asked someone to act as your mentor because you recognized the need and valued their experience.

These informal mentoring opportunities are more likely to provide people with the opportunity to discuss whole-life issues rather than restricting them to either work or non-work issues. In some organizations this might be seen as inappropriate because the view is taken that it is possible to separate and compartmentalize work and personal issues. In reality it is not possible to separate the two areas of our lives easily. Whether we like it or not, one area will impact on the other no matter how hard we try to keep them separate.

Whatever the circumstances, you are sure to gain from the experience. The main benefit of this informal approach to mentoring is that you have a choice and are in control of the process. The downside is that it can be a hit and miss affair, and this can happen without your realizing it at the time. If your organization fails to see the benefits of mentoring, you may need to carry it out informally outside working hours.

On the following pages (pp. 65–70) you will find a planning form to help you.

Conclusions

The ideal scheme is:

- supported and recognized by the organization with some formal structures and guidance notes to ensure some consistency of approach
- seen as a valid and rewarding development option by both mentors and mentees
- open to everyone who wants to take part
- voluntary, not mandatory
- able to recognize our holistic natures and accepts that personal issues can and do impact on our working lives and vice versa
- reviewed and revised regularly to ensure it continues to meet the needs of everyone involved.

PLANNING FORM

Title of scheme

Source of funding (if appropriate)

Estimate of cost (year 1)

Endorsed by (name)

What specific needs have been identified where mentoring can make a contribution?

Reproduced from *The Mentoring Manual* by Mike Whittaker and Ann Cartwright, Gower, Aldershot

Based on these needs, what are the main objectives of the scheme?

What other initiatives could mentoring be linked to?

Identify potential mentees
(include job titles, possible names, age-range, functions, departments)

Identify potential mentors
(job titles and names)

How well will potential mentors respond?

What sort of difficulties/objections can be anticipated?

How will mentors and mentee be matched?
(establish method and the name/s of final decision-maker)

What training will be provided?
(type, length, cost, internal/external)

Can our own staff deliver the training?
(specify who)

If external training providers are used, how will these be selected?

How will the training be evaluated?

How will the mentoring scheme be promoted?
(give details)

Will mentees and mentors be nominated or asked to volunteer?
(give details)

If volunteers are called for and some are not selected what actions will be taken to inform them?

Who will be responsible for administering the scheme?

What will be their main responsibilities?

Will there be a review mechanism for mentees and mentors? Yes/No
(if 'YES', give proposed details)

What is the target date to get the scheme underway?

When will the scheme be reviewed?

How will the scheme be reviewed and who will be involved?

Reproduced from *The Mentoring Manual* by Mike Whittaker and Ann Cartwright,
Gower, Aldershot

3   Key roles in mentoring

Introduction

This section reviews the key roles in mentoring and how they interrelate. In practice, except possibly where mentoring is on an entirely informal basis, these interrelationships will have considerable impact on the success of your own scheme. The main roles can be seen as:

- *Mentor* – helping someone through a significant transition/s.
- *Mentee* – the person being helped (the word itself maybe seems contrived but it's surely better than protégé!).
- *Line manager* – to whom the mentee directly reports.
- *Champion or sponsor* – person of influence who is likely to have an important bearing on the progress of the scheme particularly in the early stages.
- *Facilitator* – the organizer, the administrator, keeps the wheels oiled, reviews mentoring in the organization, likely to have a big part in the matching process.

As you read this now you may be thinking, 'I've been all of these at one time or other.' We think the book is likely to be of most interest to you when you are in the role of facilitator, either currently with the task of setting up a mentoring scheme or reviewing what you already have in place.

In various parts of the book we make reference to the growing use of mentoring in ever-changing circumstances. In the 1970s schemes in the UK may have focused on the career development of 'high flyers'. With the millennium fast approaching, as mentoring becomes more widespread values are changing at the same time. The mentor may be seen as a guide and advisor but 'a font of all knowledge' will perhaps be less acceptable to a mentee in these rapidly changing times. We will avoid making hard and fast rules because so much depends on individual circumstances. Difference in status between mentor and mentee, however, would seem to be less important today than twenty-five years ago. In addition, people are increasingly involved in co-mentoring initiatives, either as part of or independent of existing schemes.

Issues and questions

So, is difference in status of no consequence?

Picking up the point raised above, the writer feels that a difference in status is less important than it used to be. Much will depend on the objectives of the mentoring scheme, expectations of the mentee and how well the two work together whatever their respective positions in the organization. If you are the facilitator, you will in all probability have an important part to play in the selection and matching process. Clearly, you will be seeking a process which works for all concerned in your scheme (see pp. 91–97, 'The matching process').

Having set up a process that meets your needs, the second important task is to monitor the progress of the relationships. This needs to be done with some subtlety to ensure that confidentiality is preserved.

Can a line manager be both boss and mentor to the same person?

In practice this happens occasionally. But it must be difficult for all concerned. The same person acting as both line manager and mentor will have different priorities according to different circumstances. Mentees may feel themselves being pulled in different directions. The quick answer would be that ideally this situation is best avoided. It can only work where both parties are clear about the times when:

1   We are now working as line manager and report
2   We are now working as mentor and mentee.

Successful mentoring depends on openness and honesty from the two participants. This dimension presents an additional challenge to the relationship.

What makes an effective mentor?

The effective mentor demonstrates skill and support in key areas. He or she:

● has an outlook which is both positive and realistic
● is prepared to give quality time to others
● will listen and not pre-judge
● retains an interest in their own growth and development
● has a degree of self-assurance which enables them to be challenged and receive criticism (and to give it)
● is prepared for occasional feelings of discomfort.

Can a mentor also act as coach?

The short answer to this is, 'Very much so and a lot else besides'. Our previous manual, *32 Activities on Coaching and Mentoring*, contains the activity, 'Mentoring a Skills Clinic', in which we list seven key skills as follows:

● COACHING – helping to develop skills through discussion and guided activity.
● QUESTIONING – asking appropriate questions and receiving quality/ authentic responses.
● LISTENING – active listening involves giving full attention to the other speaker.
● SUMMARIZING – giving an accurate account of what has just been said.

- GIVING FEEDBACK – expressing observations and feelings with clarity and sensitivity.
- INFLUENCING – having a significant effect on the way others think and on what they do next.
- COUNSELLING – providing the support which enables people to express their feelings and consider their options.

There may be other skills that you would like to add to our list.

The conclusion is that mentoring involves using a variety of skills during what is essentially a long-term relationship. When someone is acting as a coach the activity is likely to be more specific and short term.

What sort of approaches should I make to get my ideas across to the champion of the mentoring scheme?

Having identified your possible ally you may be considering what is likely to be your best strategy to gain their support. We will look at this soon in the section, 'Influencing strategy' (see below).

Is it practical for me to be both facilitator and mentor?

Providing you have the time, it makes eminent sense for you to be a mentor as well as facilitator. You will experience at first hand the positive and at times challenging aspects of mentoring. Elsewhere in the manual we refer to the importance of discretion and confidentiality in individual mentoring relationships. As the scheme's facilitator it is vital that you are seen as a model of discretion. You are unlikely to be exposed to potential conflicting roles that the line manager/mentor might expect, as referred to earlier in this section.

4   Influencing strategy

Introduction

The situation you may face is one where you are convinced of the benefits that mentoring could bring to your organization and some of the people in it. You are aware that other initiatives have been tried in the past and you simply want to avoid another 'nine-day wonder'. If we talk about influencing – and this sometimes involves getting someone to do something they are not too keen on – you may think that this seems at odds with the supportive nature of mentoring. We feel there are times when you have to be pragmatic and go ahead to get something done in the face of possible opposition. The end justifies the means because of the longer term benefits. The issue of influencing here is considered under three headings:

1   'Selling' the concept of mentoring
2   Influencing the champion or sponsor
3   Influencing mentors and mentees, particularly where there appears to be some resistance.

It could be that everyone in the organization is sold on the idea of mentoring and you have to make very little effort to convince people about its benefits. The champion or sponsor may actually have approached you to explore the possibility of implementing a scheme. The chances are, however, that not everyone will see mentoring as the answer to all prayers.

In considering your strategy on influencing others we feel it may be helpful to consider your own influencing style, in particular taking account of your own past successes.

Selling the concept

First, think of getting people on your side:

● Who has said they want to have a mentor?
● Who will derive most benefit from mentoring?
● Who has previous experience of mentoring?
● Who has expressed an interest in becoming a mentor?

You may feel it appropriate to talk privately to those showing most interest or who are likely to be most supportive. If you can get early support from a potential champion or sponsor this could provide you with the help you need in selling the concept in the organization.

Whichever approach you adopt it will help if you have thought about main objectives, scope and benefits and so on, even if at this stage you are not able to include all the finer detail. The channels of communication you use to present an outline of the scheme will be those which from your own experience are most effective: meetings; organization publication (if you have one); notice boards; and any combination of formal and informal methods. As part of the process you may, at an early stage, seek mentors and mentees.

Influencing the champion or sponsor

There are three stages to this:

1   Establishing champions or sponsors, their expectations and responses
2   Reviewing your own preferred style and previous successes
3   Planning and presenting your case.

The champion or sponsor

- Who has real influence here?
- What are they like and how would they respond to the concept of mentoring?
- In a sentence, what am I trying to achieve?
- What are the benefits of mentoring?
- How will it fit into our culture here?
- Do I need to 'sell' the concept by developing needs or can I just present some facts?
- Could I get the champion or sponsor to reflect on personal learning experiences?
- Have they received any form of mentoring support?

My influencing style

- Do I influence through asking questions or telling?
- How successful have I been in influencing others?
- Identify recent examples where it worked well
- What did I do which resulted in my being successful?
- What can I use now to influence the champion or sponsor?
- What do I need to avoid doing?

Presenting the case

You may find the form 'Presenting My Case' (pp. 77–80) a useful tool in preparing your case for the champion or sponsor. It will help you decide whether your approach is basically one of 'tell', that is, you are giving the other person a straight presentation of the facts: the purpose of the scheme; who will be involved; time-scale, and so on.

On the other hand, the other person may be thinking something like this:

> I really don't know that much about mentoring. I need to be convinced why we should go ahead with this. Why do we need it? We've got along without it for quite some time. But I won't dismiss it out of hand. I'll listen and if it sounds right I would seriously be prepared to give it my support. But I don't want some airy-fairy ideas straight from a textbook.

Having established whether you 'tell' or 'sell', your outline of the projected mentoring scheme could cover:

- main purpose
- link to other initiatives (if appropriate)
- people involved, sections, departments where it would be most beneficial
- source of mentors
- benefits to mentees, mentors, and the organization
- how the champion or sponsor could help

- training provision
- a provisional plan for implementation with time-scale.

To help you with your influencing strategy you may wish to use the following forms. To think through your strategy, complete *Presenting my case* (Form 1) and *Strategy* (Form 2) on your own. Use *Agreed actions* (Form 3) in the discussions with your decision-maker.

PRESENTING MY CASE: FORM 1

Purpose: To establish an appropriate strategy to influence a key decision-maker.

Name of decision-maker:

Possible reactions to mentoring:

Previous mentoring experience if known:

Objections that might be raised:

Benefits of mentoring:

- for the organization

- for the mentee

- for the mentor

Why is mentoring appropriate for the organization now?

STRATEGY: FORM 2

Option 1: Presenting the straight facts

Is this my best option? Yes/No

If 'Yes', why?

Option 2: Developing the need – sample of possible questions

- Is the management team developing as well as you want?

- How well do we adapt to change?

- Which groups, sections, individuals seem to be isolated at times?

- What are the effects?

- What sort of support system might help the development of employees?

- Are we sufficiently concerned with the welfare of employees?

- How might we increase levels of motivation?

Summary of needs

Do I tend to 'tell' or 'sell'?

An example of a recent success:

From this example, what behaviour could I use to 'sell' mentoring?

AGREED ACTIONS: FORM 3

Sponsor: Facilitator:

Proposed mentoring scheme outline

- main purpose

- link to other initiatives

- scope (potential names and areas)

- source of mentors

- matching mentees and mentors (how to do this)

- training provision

- next actions by (time-scale)

Sponsor ....   Facilitator ....

Date to review actions:

Reproduced from *The Mentoring Manual* by Mike Whittaker and Ann Cartwright,
Gower, Aldershot

Influencing mentors and mentees

Earlier, reference was made to selling the concept of mentoring. Here we take this a step further and consider situations where mentoring is already in place. We focus on two particular situations:

1   You have either been told that a mentee and mentor are experiencing some difficulties in their relationship or you just sense that it is not working as well as it might.
2   You know some people whom you feel could really benefit from having a mentor but it is proving difficult to sell the idea to them.

Faced with either situation, you might find it useful to consider the strategy for influencing a champion or sponsor outlined previously in the text. Put simply this amounts to:

● find out where they stand on mentoring
● think of your preferred influencing style particularly if associated with some success
● select the approach most likely to succeed.

In Situation (1), your first step could be to get the two parties to acknowledge that they are experiencing some difficulties. This is, of course, easier if either or both of them have made the approach to you. If not, you need to tread warily because it may only be your perception. Assuming the relationship is not working out as well as it might, you can then encourage the mentee and mentor to talk through the difficulties either among themselves or with your help. By asking the right sort of questions and listening to the answers you can help them:

● review the difficulties objectively
● contract for new behaviour to improve the relationship
● if appropriate, agree the mentoring relationship should come to an end
● end positively recalling some of the benefits.

If you have access to our previous book, *32 Activities on Coaching and Mentoring*, two of the activities could be of help to you: 'Being Honest' (M 5) and 'Acknowledging Stages of Development' (M 11).

Influencing those apparently not interested

In saying that we know people who could benefit from mentoring we are perhaps in danger of being somewhat patronizing. 'We know what's good for you,' may be the message. David Clutterbuck's excellent first book on mentoring has the title, *Everyone Needs a Mentor*. So, if you are involved in the setting up, administration and review of a mentoring scheme, do you think everyone could benefit from mentoring?

The writer's own view is that the majority of people could benefit from having a mentor at some stage of their lives. This doesn't need to be part of a formal mentoring scheme. A friend, colleague or relative could fill this role. On the other hand, the writer has friends and acquaintances who, in the past, have failed to be convinced by his pro-mentoring argument. The same people have raised doubts about the benefits of counselling. For them, 'the jury's still out' on both counselling and mentoring.

The writer is also reminded of training consultants he knows who insist that they are very learner-centred. But in the next breath, instead of listening, they ram their own beliefs down the throats of their clients. People have every justification for thinking long and hard as to whether mentoring is for them.

Another important consideration is to what extent people might reject the concept of mentoring on the basis that it is a sign of weakness or failure.

- 'I'm a man and I don't need all this soft stuff.'
- 'I do a good job here. Why should I want help or guidance?'
- 'I know where I want to be. I can sort out my own career path.'
- 'I've lived on this planet for forty years. Why do I need to pour out all my innermost feelings?'
- 'What's my mentor going to tell me about myself that I don't already know?'

As the facilitator, you may occasionally be faced by those who genuinely can see no benefit to be gained from mentoring and others who express hostility because of their own fears and doubts. What do you do? Go for the easy option and involve those who do not need to be convinced? It might seem the easy way out, but if you are just getting your scheme underway it may well be expedient to go for the safer option. On the other hand, if you win over a doubting Thomas this could be an incredible success story to convince others of the merits of your scheme.

Faced with opposition or resistance to the suggestion of receiving help from a mentor you might start with some questions:

- How did you learn?
- Have you found traditional teaching/learning methods of not much help at key times in your life?
- Were there some people who really helped you when you were experiencing key changes in your life?
- Were there people you really needed at these key times and they were not to be found?
- Are there people in this organization who have the ability to help and support others?
- Have you ever thought about seeking their advice?
- Do you think we listen to each other sufficiently in this organization?
- Is there anything that could be of help to you?

These are just sample questions. Use the ones you think are appropriate and add some of your own. Then sit back and let the other person decide. Any attempt to push the benefits of mentoring with a 'hard sell' approach is likely to be counter-productive. In most cases you will gain more by using the sort of approach a mentor would adopt but do allow for an occasional exception to this rule.

You may or may not succeed. If it doesn't work, reflect on it, learn from it and move on. If you've done your homework there will be success stories elsewhere.

5 Mentoring and culture

Introduction

In this section we will try to supply answers to several questions, the relevance of which depends on whether you already have mentoring in place or are considering its implementation.

Is mentoring right for our culture? What could we do to make our mentoring scheme more effective in our existing culture? Throughout this manual we refer to the wide-ranging uses of mentoring in many different contexts.

How do planned objectives contribute to its success or failure? For example, is mentoring more likely to be successful if the main purpose of the scheme is to support career development programmes for graduates? This could be in a traditionally autocratic culture where the 'softer' mentoring approach might appear to be alien to the prevailing culture.

If you work for an international organization, will mentoring work in different cultures? An important consideration relates to the matching process and how successful the pairing of mentor and mentee can be if they come from different cultural backgrounds.

This section will consider a number of issues relating to mentoring and culture and will conclude with a questionnaire that will enable readers to focus on their specific organizations.

Two case studies

At times, do you get bored with reading how successful an organization has been in implementing the latest management technique/initiative and how well everybody has responded to the change process? You may well believe, with the writer, that today's success is tomorrow's failure, but the writer also feels that you can often learn more through failure than you can through success. The following two examples throw some light on the subject of culture.

The first example concerns a large manufacturing organization. As part of an extensive change programme involving the introduction of new production methods and management approaches, a major training and development programme was implemented. A mentoring scheme was established to support the development of people at all levels. Operating in a highly competitive business environment, the prevailing culture is described as 'macho' and 'autocratic'. In spite of great efforts the mentoring scheme failed. The conclusion could be that it failed because of the culture.

Mentoring was conducted by experienced and professional managers, which might add strength to the argument that failure was due to the effects of culture. In fact, this seems to be too simplistic a conclusion. Closer examination reveals that in a time of enormous change too much was expected of the mentoring initiative. Managers might be experienced, but if insufficient time is spent on developing their mentoring skills, it will be difficult for them to provide effective mentoring support. With other complications such as extensive redundancies, it is not surprising that the scheme failed; a case of too much, too soon in what were difficult circumstances. The prevailing culture made it difficult, but not impossible, to implement mentoring.

The second example is based on the writer's own experiences. This is not so much a case of where mentoring failed but rather where it was actually needed but never implemented. At some time in most of our lives, we take a job that does not suit us, nor are we what the organization needs. Starting employment with a training organization with excellent, well-established and universally accepted products seemed a heaven-sent opportunity. Developing business with blue-chip clients was testimony of the quality of the service provided. Somehow, however, the match did not work and both the writer and the organization felt they had made the wrong choice. What is of particular interest is that there were all sorts of contradictions in terms of the excellent programmes delivered by professional staff. On the surface these people were confident, almost arrogant but deep down some at least felt very insecure and lacked confidence. This was an organization that provided an excellent service to its customers but was incredibly inept at developing its own staff. As a newcomer, the writer, when co-delivering a programme with an experienced trainer, found it very difficult to gain credibility because of the enormous gap in product knowledge. This situation cried out for intensive coaching and mentoring support but these skills were hard to find in the organization nor was there evidence of will. No one said so, but perhaps it was a case of, 'We don't need all that soft mentoring stuff.'

Those questions again

Is it right for our culture?

You will, of course, be the best judge of this. The first example quoted confirmed that inevitably in some cultures it may prove difficult to implement successful mentoring, but the autocratic-like culture does not automatically mean that it won't work. Much depends on how you plan to implement mentoring and if you anticipate barriers as a result of traditional, unyielding values and behaviour 'a bit at a time' in the most receptive areas, this would seem to be a solution to possible resistance.

How could we make our scheme more effective?

Again, knowledge of your culture will help you to identify those areas where you would like to see improvements. You will not have a magic wand to change the culture overnight. An analysis of what is working well, what isn't, who is receptive and who is not will lead to improvement providing you gain commitment from others on the organization. (See the questionnaires at the end of this section, pp. 87–90.)

Your culture – success linked to objectives?

If you work in a very much results-driven organization, mentoring initiatives with clearly prescribed outcomes are likely to be more highly regarded than some of the less measurable benefits, such as a reduction in the turnover of graduates and improved exam results.

Mentoring in the international context

Some societies and cultures are more receptive to mentoring than others. If you are in the process of implementing mentoring on an international basis, account needs to be taken of local customs and norms. The logical approach would suggest that you start small-scale in the area you know best (presumably your own country), make a success of it and then extend it. If mentoring is not seen as an integral part of society in some cultures you may have to acknowledge this fact. The same could apply where your organization has a number of units within your own country. The time or circumstances might suggest that it is not appropriate. Start where you are likely to gain most success.

Key points

Further points for your consideration:

- The matching of mentors and mentees coming from different cultural backgrounds may appear problematical but it is possible to achieve.
- If the culture is potentially hostile, start small-scale and choose the path of least resistance.
- If your main decision-maker is seen as autocratic and unreceptive to mentoring, start elsewhere.
- There is probably hardly any organization where there is no place for mentoring. Informal mentoring takes place in the most unlikely and hostile environments, perhaps precisely because of the hostility.
- If mentoring is not as successful as you had hoped, don't conclude that, 'I knew it wouldn't work in our culture.'

Actions

The suggestion is that you take stock of the culture in your organization either:

1   To consider those cultural aspects that could contribute to a successful scheme if you are currently considering implementation
2   To review your existing scheme in the context of your prevailing culture.

You may find it useful to refer to an activity in our earlier book, *32 Activities on Coaching and Mentoring* (Gower, 1997), 'Understanding Organizational Culture'. This activity suggests that you consider how both 'formal' and 'informal' organizations operate, who has the real power and how change is brought about.

Complete whichever of the two questionnaires that follow is appropriate for your current situation to enable you to decide on your next course of action.

ASSESSING CULTURE: 1 NEW SCHEME

How would I describe the culture?

Are there contradictions between the formal/informal organization? Yes/No

Examples

Formal

Policy statements
Hierarchy
Business plans
Formal meetings

Informal

Informal groups
Power
Atmosphere
Get-togethers

If there are contradictions, specify

In what ways might these get in the way of effective mentoring?

If they might help, specify

In what ways would mentoring be of benefit?

Who in particular would benefit?

In selling the benefits of mentoring what objections might be anticipated and who might object?

Actions to be taken: specify actions and names

Now   1 month   3 months

Reproduced from *The Mentoring Manual* by Mike Whittaker and Ann Cartwright,
Gower, Aldershot

ASSESSING CULTURE: 2 EXISTING SCHEME

How would I describe the culture?

Are there contradictions between the formal/informal organization? Yes/No

Examples

Formal   *Informal*

Policy statements   Informal groups
Hierarchy   Power
Business plans   Atmosphere
Formal meetings   Get-togethers

If there are contradictions, specify

In what ways do these hinder the mentoring scheme?

Do they help in any way? Specify

What impact does culture have on the mentoring scheme?

What improvements could be made?

Actions to be taken: specify with names

Now   1 month   3 months

6   The matching process

Introduction

Successful mentoring is dependent on how well mentors and mentees work together. This is an obvious statement no doubt, but if you are involved in the setting up and/or facilitation of a scheme careful thought should be given to the mentor/mentee matching process. Aim for something that fits in with the main objectives and scope of your particular scheme. This is not to say that there will be perfect matches each time. It is a question, however, of keeping your finger on the pulse to encourage possible changes if relationships appear not to be working (see the mentoring profile forms at the end of this section).

In this section we examine the sort of issues arising and concerns you might have regarding the matching process. We are not attempting to provide an answer to everything but at least present you with some guidelines. We hope that at the end you will have enough information to establish a strategy that works best for you. One thing that makes mentoring so interesting is that you will come across some surprising matches that work well contrary to expectations.

Issues and questions

- How do you decide your selection strategy?
- What sort of criteria should you use as part of the matching process?
- Does a mentor have to be proficient in the mentee's discipline?
- As a facilitator do you make a decision yourself or do you involve others?
- Should the mentors and mentees have similar personalities?
- Can the mentor be at a lower level in the hierarchy than the mentee?
- Would mentoring be more effective if mentors come from outside the organization?
- Should mentees choose their mentors?
- Should mentors have a choice of mentees?
- Is there a place for 'natural selection'?
- How do you deal with people who want to be either mentors or mentees but for various reasons are not selected?

Response to issues and questions

This is an attempt to address the issues and questions listed above. One important proviso is that these are just our thoughts and you will be aware of what most suits your own organization. At the end of this section you will decide the strategy best suited to your individual situation.

The ideas expressed here relate primarily to a formal mentoring scheme. Issues such as 'natural selection' may occur as a result of a request to someone to be a mentor outside the context of a formal mentoring scheme. (This does not imply, however, that 'natural selection' cannot take place within formal mentoring.) In planning your mentoring scheme and the implications for the matching process, logically a good starting point is to think of the objectives of the scheme and who are the potential mentees and mentors. Under 'Actions' below we describe four options for you to consider. These are concerned with who makes the decision and the degree of logic or intuition about the matching process. There are no hard and fast rules to guarantee a successful match each time.

Regarding relative position within an organization's hierarchy, traditionally the mentor would have been expected to be on at least the same or even higher level. This may be changing but much will depend on expectations and scope of the scheme. Graduates receiving support as part of their development programme would expect to have a more senior employee as mentor. Even in this situation there is now probably a case to consider someone as a mentor who has recently experienced both the highs and lows of the development programme. As a mentee seeking support in professional development again the expectation might be of working with a mentor who has at least the equivalent professional qualification. This may not always be the case, however, and effective and supportive mentoring may outweigh a reliance on academic or professional qualifications.

Two final issues to consider. First, selecting mentors from outside an organization can have its advantages and disadvantages. Someone to challenge long-established practices can help mentees re-visit their own beliefs and values that may be restricted 'politically' by accepted norms. On the other hand, the mentoring relationship may take longer to develop as the mentor becomes familiar with the culture. The second issue is that following the matching process, those people not selected either as mentors or mentees need to be given a clear explanation of the reasons for this. This has to be handled sensitively by the facilitator. Those not selected today could well be involved at some future date. Feelings of exclusivity could also undermine the potential success of the mentoring scheme.

Actions

The following are some of the actions you might wish to consider if your role is to act as facilitator of a mentoring scheme. We can think of four options for the matching process. You may well be able to add some of your own. The four are:

1   The mentee makes the decision. This could be based on some form of profiling.
2   The mentor makes the decision or at least asks the question, 'Would you like me to become your mentor?' In an informal context, the potential mentor would no doubt present this in a much less formal way.
3   The decision is taken by someone other than the mentees or mentors. If you

are the facilitator this could well be part of your role. More than one person could be involved in this decision. You may be comparing mentee and mentor profiles.

4   Mentees and mentors get together and make their own choice.

Establishing your mentoring strategy

Key stages are as follows:

- Clarify objectives and scope.
- Think of all those special circumstances that could make or break the scheme.
- Establish your matching strategy.
- Introduce some form of profiling to match mentors and mentees. (See sample forms on pp. 94–97.)
- If it is not a case of self-select decide who will make the decisions.
- Establish a mechanism to review the progress of mentoring relationships, monitor the success of matching and be prepared to change strategy if necessary.
- Ensure those not selected receive clear explanations leaving the door open for their future involvement and commitment.

MENTORING PROFILE FORM – MENTOR

Name:

Describe key events in your life

What would a partner, close friend or relative say about you?

What are your values? What's really important to you?

Reproduced from *The Mentoring Manual* by Mike Whittaker and Ann Cartwright,
Gower, Aldershot

What are your main interests?

Why are you interested in mentoring?

What skills do you have which would help you as a mentor?

Signed: Date:

MENTORING PROFILE FORM – MENTEE

Name:

Describe key events in your life

What would a partner, close friend or relative say about you?

What are your values? What's really important to you?

What are your main interests?

How do you feel you might benefit from mentoring?

What skills do you think a mentor should have?

Signed: Date:

Reproduced from *The Mentoring Manual* by Mike Whittaker and Ann Cartwright,   *97*
Gower, Aldershot

7 Training

Introduction

Earlier in this chapter (pp. 62–64) reference was made to informal mentoring and so the reader may wish to ask the question, 'If it happens in an informal, haphazard sort of way, do you really need to train someone how to mentor? Isn't it a matter of either being able to mentor or not, as the case may be?' Another similar line of thinking is that some people are born leaders, others not. So why spend all that money on management development? We believe it is important to train both mentors and managers because we feel the philosophy of 'sink or swim' is not conducive to an effective performance either as a manager or mentor.

Accepting that abilities will vary and some people will find it easier to deal with the transition from say machine operator to supervisor, why not make life easier for them by giving them some training? Throwing people in at the deep end may work for some but not for everyone. Formal mentoring in organizations is a relatively new concept and those who get involved are likely to find themselves expected to do something outside the context of their normal job. Another interesting thing is that you can never be sure who will actually take to mentoring. Someone considered eminently suited to mentoring may actually find it difficult or have doubts themselves. Even a fairly brief training programme will provide the opportunity, in most cases at least, to decide who really wants to mentor.

You may have to face the objections about the cost of training and people's availability to attend training courses. It is worth bearing in mind that you are unlikely to need extensive training programmes to familiarize mentors with both your own mentoring scheme and the necessary skills. Hard to be too precise but something like a two-day workshop should enable people to feel sufficiently confident to start mentoring. After that they will learn as they go along.

Funds even for brief training programmes, however, are not always available and you may have to do the best you can in difficult circumstances. You may be the scheme's facilitator/administrator but perhaps you can also take on the role of trainer. Below are some ideas to start you on the journey if you are going to train potential mentors.

What sort of areas should be covered on a workshop?

The very basics could run something like this:

- the role of mentor
- details of your scheme
- developing mentoring skills (plenty of practice)
- building confidence (through the skills practice and feedback)

More details on designing a workshop

The classic starting point must be that you design an event that meets the needs of delegates. For an in-house programme this shouldn't present you with undue difficulties because you know the people and can develop something to tie in with both individual needs and those of your prospective mentors.

In Chapter 5 we present details on a workshop we ran in Birmingham. You may find some useful material there to help you with the design of your own workshop. We need to point out, however, that this was a one-day 'open' event consisting of a combination of familiarization with the concept of mentoring and skills training. As delegates came from a number of organizations it was quite difficult to design a programme to meet the specific needs of people coming from different backgrounds and with varying levels of experience. You will be able to give your delegates details of your own specific mentoring scheme and tailor the workshop accordingly.

We think you won't go far wrong if the structure of your training programme looks something like this:

1 Understanding the mentoring role
2 An outline of your scheme to include main objectives and scope
3 The phases of a mentoring relationship from uncertain beginning to end
4 How do people learn? (the various learning styles)
5 Identifying the main skills associated with mentoring and practising these, for example:

- questioning
- listening
- summarizing
- counselling

6 Dealing with delegates' doubts and uncertainties
7 Agreeing actions to set up individual mentoring sessions.

Given you have an outline for your programme, what sort of things are likely to contribute to a successful event?

Essential ingredients

- a relaxed learning environment
- delegates who want to learn
- the opportunity to practise mentoring skills (frequently)
- a tutor who doesn't just 'show and tell'
- the opportunity to give and receive feedback
- increasing self-awareness
- building confidence
- preserving confidentiality.

If you think about this list, do you see a parallel with an effective mentoring relationship? If you are responsible for running a mentoring session you can expect your delegates to want to be treated in the same way as if they were mentees. So, there's no place for, 'I'll just let them make this mistake so I can tell them where they've gone wrong.' Do you know trainers who still persist in this approach?

However difficult it might prove to get your organization to agree to investing in time and money to carry out mentoring training, do what you can to ensure that you have something in place. If this is going to call on your ability to influence others refer to pages 73–83.

Finally, some organizations are prepared to run training sessions for mentees, sometimes alongside mentors, sometimes separately. You may wish to consider doing this as well.

8   Administration

Introduction

Earlier under 'Planning' (pp. 58–64) we recommended that you take careful account of those key people who can make or break your scheme. Formal and informal approaches were discussed as was the use of a pilot scheme. We also considered the actual scope of mentoring schemes.

Having set up mentoring in your organization you need also to ensure that the administration is of the right calibre to achieve success for your scheme. Here we explore briefly the part played by the facilitator.

Facilitator's role

In this manual reference has been made to the crucial role that effective mentors will play in the success of a mentoring scheme; they can be described as a long-term guide, counsellor and friend. The facilitator/administrator has an equally crucial role. Apart from a vital contribution to the setting up of the scheme, they are likely to be involved in the day-to-day issues of organizing training, arranging meetings between mentors and mentees, the matching process, review and support group meetings, and so on. But of course there's much more to it. Dealing with what might be termed the 'nuts and bolts' of mentoring is one thing; keeping an eagle eye on the whole process is another.

The most effective facilitators/administrators are probably 'hands-on' for the more mundane aspects. For other tasks they may be seen to play a significant but at the same time unobtrusive role in promoting good relationships within the scheme. They:

- can sense when mentors and mentees are experiencing difficulties
- act as advisors/counsellors at appropriate times
- can be trusted by all concerned
- are seen to be discreet
- maintain effective links with the scheme's champion/sponsor
- show good awareness of the mentee–mentor–line manager relationship
- monitor the progress of the scheme objectively
- are able to come up with sound ideas for improving the existing scheme.

It sounds like the salesman, administrator, counsellor and friend all rolled into one!

9   Setting up support networks

Introduction

As part of the ongoing support for your mentoring scheme you might find it useful to set up some support networks for both mentors and mentees. The process listed below can be used to assist both the mentor and mentee to identify the type of support they need and want and to explore ways of gaining this support. (This is an adaptation of the activity 'Developing Support Networks', from *32 Activities for Coaching and Mentoring*.)

The process

The key aim of the process is to assist both the mentor and mentee to:

- identify their present and future support needs
- review the range and type of support currently available to them
- take the actions needed to improve the range and type of support they might need in the future.

The process works in the following way and can be done individually or as part of a development workshop:

- Complete the forms at the end of this section
- Arrange to discuss your responses with your mentor or partner at your next session or at the appropriate time in the workshop.
- Your mentor or partner should be encouraging you to be specific about your needs. It is important to be very clear about what you want.
- Your mentor or partner should work with you to complete the action plan (p. 106). If you are working with a mentor, this action plan can be reviewed at a later date to check on progress.
- Review the key learning points from the activity, for example:

– What were your feelings about the activity?
– What were the key learning points for you?
– What surprises were there for you?

DEVELOPING SUPPORT GROUPS: 1

What type of support do I have at present?

What type of support do I want/need in the future?

Who gives me this support?

– now?

– in the future?

Reproduced from *The Mentoring Manual* by Mike Whittaker and Ann Cartwright,   *103*
Gower, Aldershot

DEVELOPING SUPPORT GROUPS: 2

1   What are my unmet support needs?

2   How can I give myself support in these areas?

3   Who do I know who can give me support in these areas?

4   Have I asked for this support before and if so what happened?

   Reproduced from *The Mentoring Manual* by Mike Whittaker and Ann Cartwright, Gower, Aldershot

5   What 'support' groups do I belong to at present inside or outside work?

6   Will the organization encourage me to set up a 'support group' at work?

7   Who might be interested in this group?

8   Who will I need to speak to about setting up a group?

9   Am I prepared to do this?

ACTION PLAN

1   The support I am looking for in the future is:

2   The people who can give me this support are:

3   The actions I need to take are:

4   My time-table for these actions is:

Reproduced from *The Mentoring Manual* by Mike Whittaker and Ann Cartwright,
Gower, Aldershot

10   Monitoring and evaluation

Introduction

This section focuses on monitoring and evaluation of the mentoring process. It covers the following three areas:

1   Measuring against an effective mentoring model
2   Reviewing individual mentoring relationships
3   Broadcasting success.

This section does not attempt to provide all the answers. It simply aims to provide some guidelines and examples around the important question of monitoring and evaluation.

Why is monitoring and evaluation important?

As with many things in life, we need to look back regularly and review what, why and how things have happened in order to recognize and acknowledge our successes and failures. For example, as children we continually monitored our growth progress against a measured mark on the wall or against a height chart. Many people use their bathroom scales to continuously monitor their weight losses and gains. We use bank statements to review our ongoing financial situation. We carry out these forms of monitoring and evaluation on a continuous and often unconscious basis. It is through this process that we can keep an eye on our progress in a variety of different and complex situations.

In the same way organizational processes need to be continuously reviewed and revised if they are to remain effective. As a development process, mentoring needs to be continuously reviewed and revised to ensure that the development needs of both the mentee and the mentor are met.

Measuring against an effective mentoring model

Within your own organization, when you set up your mentoring scheme you will have had some key objectives and outcomes that you hope to achieve through the mentoring process. In order to ensure that you have met these objectives and outcomes you will need to carry out systematic and regular reviews of your mentoring scheme. This needs to be done not only to ensure that the scheme continues to meet the needs of all the participants. It needs to be done to continuously demonstrate the 'business case' for the scheme and a return on investment.

Whatever the reason, it is important that the review looks at the scheme from three perspectives:

1   Benefits to the mentor
2   Benefits to the mentee
3   Benefits to the organization.

The reviews can be done in a number of ways. For example, they could include the use of review questionnaires like those on pp. 112–115, one-to-one interviews with a random sample of mentors and mentees, review workshops that bring together groups of mentors and mentees to examine the benefits and key learning points gained from the mentoring process. A combination of all three could be employed. The important point is that you monitor and evaluate the scheme on a regular basis.

Reviewing individual mentoring relationship

In addition to you as the facilitator monitoring and evaluating the overall programme, each partnership within the scheme should also be encouraged to carry out a regular review. Individual reviews can also be done in a number of ways. For example, a partnership might agree to take 5–10 minutes at the beginning or end of each session to review and reflect on that session and decide what, if any, changes need to be made to the process, structure, format and so on. Alternatively, a partnership might agree to using every third or fourth session as a review meeting rather than a mentoring meeting. This would provide an opportunity to reflect on past sessions and explore what needed to be done differently or better in future sessions. Again, it is possible to use questionnaires to carry out individual reviews.

Individual reviews are likely to focus more on the format, structure and content of the process as well as exploring the three perspectives identified above. In addition, individual reviews need to explore if and when either party outgrows the other. If the relationship is to remain beneficial to both the mentor and mentee, both need to learn to recognize and acknowledge when it is time to move on and remember that the mentoring relationship is not a life-time commitment.

Broadcasting successes

One of the key organizational benefits of regularly monitoring and evaluating your mentoring scheme is that it will provide you with an excellent source of anecdotes and case studies that can be used to *broadcast the successes*. This is especially useful if you introduced mentoring on a pilot basis.

The best way to promote and encourage wider participation in the scheme is to use real examples of the benefit gained from real people. This was demonstrated in the organizational case study outlined earlier in the book. The 'Scheme Champion' participants on the mentoring scheme sold the scheme to other colleagues creating a snowball effect. As a result he had very little 'selling' to do in order to expand the scheme.

Other ways of broadcasting your success could include articles in staff newsletters written by participants; inviting existing participants to share their experiences at your next introductory workshop; encouraging mentees to become mentors. There may be many other ways that you can think of that would better suit the needs and culture of your organization.

In carrying out evaluation, the reader may find it useful to refer to the forms included in The Midlands Engineering Company Study in Chapter 2 (pp. 29–38).

Conclusion

Although the mentoring process largely takes place behind closed doors and involves two people it can still have an impact, both positively and negatively, across the organization. Like all relationships, the mentoring relationship can and does go through some bad patches that can cause a great deal of heartache and pain if they are not given the right levels of support at the right time.

By building regular monitoring systems and procedures into the process from the start, you can make the necessary corrective adjustments at the right time, in the right place and in the right way.

11   What can go wrong

Introduction

While the use of mentoring may be increasing there may be times when you ask yourself, 'Why ever did I want to get involved with all this?' Hopefully, the good times will outweigh the bad. The important thing is to remember the learning opportunities that those difficulties actually present. In this section we list a number of difficulties, include some examples in more depth, and refer to key sections earlier in the text to provide you with some guidance on possible solutions. As a process the following may help:

1   Define the problem
2   Establish the main cause
3   Design and implement the solution
4   Review.

Difficulties

These are listed under *people*, *objectives and review*, and *mechanics* but there is, of course, considerable overlap.

People

- some don't want to be mentored
- some don't want to be mentors
- negative reactions from others not involved in the scheme
- those who could gain most are not involved
- breaches of confidentiality.

Objectives and review

- lack of clarity regarding objectives
- lack of clarity on key roles
- no real attempt made to evaluate the scheme
- a failure to learn from both successes and failures
- success isn't publicized.

Mechanics

- loss of momentum to the scheme
- matching process doesn't seem to work
- lack of support outside the mentor/mentee relationship
- mentor/mentee meetings don't take place or are cancelled at short notice
- insufficient training; people 'sink or swim'
- mentoring is used in isolation of other initiatives when benefits would result from some form of integration.

Potential problem areas

We now look at six potential problem areas in more detail.

Problem area 1 – The mentoring scheme is losing momentum

Your scheme may have seemed quite successful during the early stages. Of late, however, you feel enthusiasm for it has diminished; nobody ever seems to talk about mentoring, people are not coming forward asking to be mentors or be mentored. You hear that appointments have been cancelled at short notice and you start to think that mentoring may be seen as a fad now in decline.

It may be that issues at work in general have been particularly difficult and this colours your judgement on all manner of things. So, it's a question of thinking, 'Have I got it right?' The process we suggest here is simply to test your own feelings with the perception of others and to take any corrective action to put life back into the scheme. In extreme circumstances you may feel that the 'natural life' of your scheme has come to an end.

You may decide to review the scheme on a one-to-one basis but it may well be more appropriate to get collective thoughts via a review meeting. On pp. 112–115, you will find a review form which you could use to summarize the findings and to plan for change. The process is likely to be:

1 Do we feel the scheme is okay as it is?
2 Do we need to revise objectives and scope?
3 If 'yes', what are the suggested changes?
4 Clarify who does what and when.
5 Has the scheme outlived its usefulness?
6 If this is considered the case in its present form, could it still be usefully extended to others?
7 If it's felt that the scheme has served its purpose, what form should the winding down process take?

If changes are thought necessary, some areas to consider include:

● methods of communication
● matching
● administration
● training.

You may also find it useful to refer to 'Measuring Success', an activity in *32 Activities on Coaching and Mentoring*. This activity suggests the following nine criteria against which the success of a mentoring scheme can be measured:

1 Meetings
2 Objectives
3 Expectations (in the mentoring relationship) are met even if they change
4 Awareness of the stages in mentoring
5 Actions taken
6 Benefits
7 Behaviour
8 Regular progress review
9 Confidentiality is maintained.

MENTORING REVIEW MEETING NOTES

Date:

Scheme objectives:

Names of mentees:

Names of mentors:

Overall perception of the scheme (thoughts of the group):

Reproduced from *The Mentoring Manual* by Mike Whittaker and Ann Cartwright, Gower, Aldershot

Benefits to:

Mentors   Mentees   Organization

What has proved to be most difficult?

What actions have been taken to overcome these?

Are the objectives of the scheme clearly defined and appropriate?

If 'No' specify changes

Reproduced from *The Mentoring Manual* by Mike Whittaker and Ann Cartwright,   *113*
Gower, Aldershot

Is the scope of the scheme as extensive as it needs to be?

If 'No' specify changes

Is this considered to be the end of the 'natural life' of the scheme?

If 'Yes', describe the reasons for this

Assuming the group feels mentoring should continue, what areas for improvement are suggested?
(e.g. communication, matching, training, administration)

Agreed actions

By whom   When

Area 1

Area 2

Area 3

Area 4

Problem area 2 – Adverse reactions to mentoring from a line manager

On rare occasions a line manager may also be a mentor to one of his or her subordinates. Here we consider the situation where there might be some conflict in the tripartite relationship between the line manager, the mentor and the mentee. Inevitably there are different expectations and objectives within this relationship. For example, in a manufacturing environment the line manager could be a production manager under pressure to meet tight deadlines. The line manager's style is to impose similar pressure on his subordinate, a supervisor. The latter's mentor sees the adverse effect on his/her mentee, who in response to the production manager comes up with a series of ' quick fixes'. The supervisor would like to be able to avoid repeated fire-fighting situations and to take a longer-term view of where he/she is. In discussion with the mentor, the mentee feels the need to do things differently but is constrained by day-to-day pressures.

In considering possible difficulties from the tripartite relationship, our first thoughts are that the reader is the facilitator wishing to play a part in reconciling the differences. But if instead you are the line manager, mentee or mentor we hope there may be some ideas here to help you resolve this situation.

As a facilitator, you may have a hunch that there are difficulties in a particular relationship. On the other hand, mentor, mentee or the line manager may have approached you. The following process is suggested as a way of analysing the situation objectively and of improving the relationship:

1   An objective assessment of the tripartite relationship as *you* see it. (Use the form on pp. 117–120.)
2   Summarize the difficulties in the relationship as you see them. (If none are identified or these seem minimal you need to consider how you approach the three parties, if the approach came from them.)
3   Set up formal or informal meetings:
    ● informal – individually
    ● formal – all three.
4   Talk through differences and agree actions (possible contracting)
    ● 'More of, less of, the same' (behaviour and actions for all three).
5   Agree review mechanism with dates.

TRIPARTITE MENTORING RELATIONSHIPS

The purpose of this form is to contribute to an objective assessment of the relationships between mentee, mentor and line manager. Account is taken of the objectives of the organization's mentoring scheme.

MENTEE

LINE MANAGER   MENTOR

Objectives of the mentoring scheme:

Departmental objectives:

Mentee

What I expect from my line manager:

How my mentor can help me:

The difficulties I am experiencing are:

Changes that would help me:

Reproduced from *The Mentoring Manual* by Mike Whittaker and Ann Cartwright,
Gower, Aldershot

Line manager

What I expect from the mentee:

How the mentor can help:

The difficulties I am experiencing:

Changes that would help me:

Reproduced from *The Mentoring Manual* by Mike Whittaker and Ann Cartwright,   *119*
Gower, Aldershot

Mentor

What I expect from the line manager:

The difficulties experienced by the mentee:

Changes that would help both mentee and line manager:

What I can do to help resolve any difficulties:

Problem area 3 – Struggling to get mentoring off the ground

You could be the human resource specialist or the person with a key role of facilitator for your organization's mentoring scheme. Somehow you feel that the time is right for some form of mentoring initiative. You may even have been told, 'Go ahead and get something in place.' This may seem fine but you sense most responses appear to be lukewarm and somewhat indifferent. If you work in the human resources function this may be regarded as 'Another initiative from HR just like appraisal where you sit down every year and have this meaningless review for half an hour between the boss and subordinate, fill in the appraisal form and send it back to HR.'

To summarize, you may be faced with some inertia from different levels in the organization and yet you feel there would be real benefits from an effective mentoring scheme.

The following process will help you work through this situation and you may choose to make use of the process review form on pp. 123–127. There are also a few golden rules at the end which may help with the process. You may well want to add some of your own.

1   Personal reflections
Why do we need mentoring? In what ways would it help? How would it fit in with the culture here? Who specifically would benefit from it? Why does there appear to be this inertia?

2   Own decision
Well, have I got it right? Should I pursue this issue? If 'no', who do I need to go back to and how do I convey my decision?

3   The scheme – first take
This assumes you want to go ahead. You may wish to consider provisional objectives: who could be mentors and mentees; whether or not it is appropriate to tie in with other initiatives such as management development; the potential areas for resistance/objections and sources of power and influence.

4   Testing ideas with others
Decide who will give you good feedback on your initial thoughts, make the approach and note possible amendments to the scheme.

5   Initial draft of scheme
Produce a summary of the mentoring scheme to include objectives, a list of potential participants, matching process, potential benefits to the organization, mentees and mentors and thoughts on how training needs could be met.

6   Influencing – strategy and implementation
Decide whom you need to approach and the appropriate strategy. This could be

more than just the person with most influence. You may wish to talk to people who are likely to benefit from the scheme either as mentors or mentees. For guidance on the most effective way to influence others you may wish to refer to pp. 73–83.

7   Final design of scheme

Your final design will include those areas listed under (5) above with amendments. Personal knowledge of those you have presented your ideas to will dictate the amount of detail given under (6).

8   Implementation and evaluation

As at the outset you envisaged some indifference or inertia it may well make sense to go for a small-scale pilot mentoring scheme. Some other golden rules that might help are:

- ensure objectives and scope are well communicated and understood
- include adequate training provision
- be a mentor yourself (if possible)
- set milestones for the scheme
- monitor mentoring relationships but without breaching confidentiality
- encourage people to keep appointments
- gain commitment from others
- extend scope to others as the scheme becomes more successful.

MENTORING – PROCESS REVIEW

1   Personal reflections

Why mentoring for us?

Specific ways in which it could help

Who would benefit (functions, jobs, named individuals)

How might it relate to our culture?

Does there seem to be indifference towards mentoring?

What are the reasons for this?

Reproduced from *The Mentoring Manual* by Mike Whittaker and Ann Cartwright,   *123*
Gower, Aldershot

2 First review

Do I take it further or abandon the idea now? Yes/No

If 'No', what are the reasons for this?

If 'No', who do I need to approach and what do I convey to them?

3   First take

If 'Yes', the following areas to consider are:

Main objectives

Mentees

Mentors

Other related initiatives

Who might resist and why?

Who would be a useful source of power/influence?

4   Testing my ideas

With whom should I test my ideas?

What were their reactions and what might I reconsider?

5   Initial draft

This will include:

- objectives
- participants (provisional)
- matching process
- benefits to organization, mentees, mentors
- training provision.

6   Influencing

Who will I approach? What is the preferred way to influence them?

What feedback did I get? What do I need to reconsider?

7 Final design of scheme (use separate page/s if needed)

8 Implementation (dates and key stages)

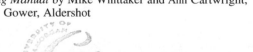

Problem area 4 – The impact of a merger or takeover on your scheme

Your mentoring scheme may have been in place for a few months. It started as a pilot scheme and because of some early success you were intending to extend the scope. Out of the blue an announcement was made of a takeover by an American Mid-West company. You understand that their management style tends to be autocratic and they have a reputation for asset stripping. You are wondering, 'Is there going to be any place for mentoring in the new set-up?' In the past mentoring has been a useful support mechanism in the development of supervisors and managers. Your organization has relied on a democratic style of management with wide acceptance of total quality.

What might you do faced with a potentially highly political situation? It is probably a question of trying to do the best you can in a difficult situation. The background to mentoring in the United States of America would suggest much of it was, in the 1970s, targeted at 'fast tracking' associated with the development of high flyers. In recent years, as in the UK, mentoring in the USA has become much more widespread and extended, and used for a variety of purposes. If we assume with this particular example that mentoring is a relatively unknown quantity, some of the following steps may contribute to its survival and growth:

1   Assuming your champion or sponsor has survived the takeover, enlist their help in your campaign.

2   Review the scheme and focus on successes, drawing up a list of benefits to the organization, the mentees and mentors.

3   You are now likely to be going through a substantial change process. Establish the ways in which the scheme could contribute to this process.

4   Stress the link to management development. The new masters may well be proclaiming, 'People are our greatest asset.' This is an opportunity to contribute to manpower, succession planning and levels of motivation; the latter may take a knock as shock waves go through the organization (although this is not always the case).

5   Enlist the support of others who can demonstrate the benefits from the scheme.

6   Plan your campaign carefully and adopt an appropriate influencing style. (See earlier section on 'Influencing strategy', pp. 73–83.)

Just hope it works!

Problem area 5 – Difficulties in relationships from others' perceptions

Because only a minority of people may be directly involved in mentoring in an organization, the following sometimes happens:

- The mentoring role is misunderstood.
- Cross-gender mentoring gives rise to speculation.
- Mentor and mentee experience unease about the perception of others.

You might be the mentee or mentor experiencing situations like these or, alternatively, as a facilitator you may be aware of the difficulties in a particular relationship arising from others' perceptions. The following consists of a process to enable the parties involved to work through these difficulties. The facilitator may play a supportive role if required. If so, the facilitator needs to show empathy but also to tread warily.

Method

1 Either party introduces the subject of others' perceptions and checks out the response and general feelings about the situation.
2 Share personal benefits and learning opportunities that have been gained from the mentoring relationship. If there is some difference of opinion here, the problem might not be the perception of others but rather the quality of the relationship.
3 Share time equally to express concerns, give examples of the perceptions and the effect they have.
4 Explore the possible reasons for others' perceptions.
5 Having shared respective feelings decide the next course of action from one of the following options:

- No further action needed. The sharing of feelings has been sufficient with the conclusion that what others may feel has no negative effect on the mentoring relationship.

- Share your feelings or misgivings with the mentoring scheme's facilitator or champion. It could be that others involved in mentoring have experienced similar difficulties. If general rumours and misconceptions are as a result of the way the scheme was set up, suggest appropriate corrective action.

- Discuss your feelings at your mentoring support group (assuming you have one).

- In extreme cases it may be decided to talk through the situation with the party who has expressed hostility or negative feelings. This might require third party help and should be handled with extreme caution (likely to result in a response of surprise and denial).

6 Review the activity. The conclusion may be that the sharing of feelings has been sufficient in itself, that the process has strengthened the relationship and contributed to individual learning.

Throughout this process it is vital that mentee and mentor are in full agreement at each stage and share feelings honestly and openly.

This activity appears in full in *32 Activities on Coaching and Mentoring*.

Problem area 6 – 'Should I really be acting almost as a counsellor?'

Of all the aspects of mentoring this one is subject to most debate and potentially can lead to most disagreement. The statement itself suggests some feeling of discomfort. Perhaps it's not all that reassuring to say it, but most mentors will experience difficult emotions. It could be at the start of the relationship with some feeling of uncertainty or trepidation; it might be at the end as you prepare to say goodbye for the last time after perhaps two years together.

The following is the opinion of the writer who acknowledges that others very experienced in mentoring will not agree with him. Let's now take a look at one definition of mentoring:

> Providing guidance, support and practical help through life crises or into new stages of development

You may feel that this is very close to what you understand as the concept of counselling. Trying to distinguish between the two, we would say that mentoring is helping someone make the most of themselves through increased self-knowledge, and that counselling is helping someone to resolve problems. We admit this is a thin dividing line and we could talk all night about definitions. Whatever we agree or disagree on, emotions have a big part to play in the supportive role provided by the mentor. A mentor can't simply say, 'Well, by our next meeting you will have agreed whether or not you'll take up that career in the Army' and ignore the fact that his mentee was in tears at the start of their meeting. A simplistic example perhaps, but the mentoring role can't be neatly divided into someone to help with something like a decision on a career move and someone to deal with the mentee's emotions.

Of course it's not as simple as that. First of all, if you think it will be difficult for you to lend a sympathetic ear when your mentee seems to be quite emotional, then mentoring may not be for you. Secondly, much as you would like to help the mentee, situations may occur for which you haven't the required skills and some form of referral is the only possible step. In this situation you must be the judge of when you need to refer. The temptation to stay with it when you are clearly out of your depth must be avoided.

You may also be faced with the difficult situation where facts of an extremely delicate nature come to light. For example, evidence of child abuse could mean it is impossible to preserve the usual anonymity and confidentiality of the mentoring relationship.

In conclusion, there are times when circumstances dictate that you act as counsellor.

II Suggestions for effective mentoring – a summary of the 11 key areas

As we said in Chapter 1, this chapter can be described as 'weighty'. There should be enough here to give you some ideas as to how you might set up mentoring or, alternatively, how you might review your existing scheme. We appreciate, however, it might help if we break this down a little bit more. First of all, under each of the 11 key areas we try to give you what we considered to be the two or three most significant factors per item.

Secondly, we reduce this number to what we call a 'Super eight' which you could use if you run a workshop on mentoring. We have also put these eight points on one page so that you can turn it into a transparency, assuming you agree with our own findings (see p. 134).

We present these in the same sequence of key areas.

1   Setting objectives

- Describe what the scheme is about but not in a way to inhibit those involved.
- Don't keep people in the dark about the main purpose of the scheme.
- Review objectives periodically. The initial ones may restrict the potential to extend the scope or may no longer be totally relevant.

2   Planning the introduction of a programme

- Think initially of success through a small-scale/pilot start.
- Ask yourself who is likely to benefit most and plan accordingly.

3   Key roles in mentoring

- Make sure the main players have some indication of what is expected of them without dotting all the 'I's' and crossing all the 'T's'.
- Think of the tripartite relationship and the role of the line manager, but don't have the line manger acting as a mentor to one of his/her own staff.
- The mentor does not necessarily have to be this infallible, wise owl of high status in the organization.
- A good champion/sponsor is an important ally.

4   Influencing strategy

- You may have to work hard to influence others because logic isn't always persuasive.
- Adopt an influencing style that works and tailor it according to individual responses. Think of what you do well but adapt it to suit the purpose.
- Accept that some people don't like mentoring for various reasons. It might be difficult to find out why this is.

5   Mentoring and culture

- To be successful go for objectives which initially at least fit the organization's prevailing culture.
- If mentoring doesn't seem to work don't put it all down to the culture.
- If you think it may be difficult to get mentoring accepted in your culture think of potential *benefits* to organization, mentee and mentor. Sell these benefits to people with real influence.

6   The matching process

- Good matches do not necessarily come from similar personalities but some common ground in terms of interests, etc. is likely to help relationships in the early stages.
- If as a facilitator you feel a match really isn't working, offer your help but with some degree of subtlety.
- Don't neglect those who expressed interest but for various reasons haven't been selected. Decide what you need to say to them.

7   Training

- Provided you have the budget, invest in training. Remember a person highly proficient in their own field may find mentoring difficult without some form of training.
- Set training objectives and measure the success of the training.

8   Administration

- As a facilitator keep a check on appointments to ensure mentees and mentors are meeting as agreed. Review individual mentoring relationships but without being intrusive.

- Maintain effective links with the scheme's champion or sponsor (if you have one).

9 Setting up support networks

- If at all possible encourage the setting up of a support network which may involve mentors or mentees or both.
- Maintain confidentiality within mentoring relationships but use the network as a potential source of learning opportunities.

10 Monitoring and evaluation

- Monitor progress of individual mentoring relationships on a regular basis but preserve confidentiality.
- Review the mentoring scheme's overall progress against objectives.
- Encourage the implementation of changes in line with needs arising from the evaluation.

11 What can go wrong?

- Accept there will be difficulties and mistakes but learn from them.
- If there do appear to be problems, see if others perceive it as you do. Your misgivings may be unwarranted.

The super eight

1   Start small-scale and build on success.
2   Clearly define the scheme's main purpose and scope.
3   Influence the right people.
4   Invest in training.
5   Encourage effective matches.
6   Monitor progress.
7   Broadcast success (but preserve confidentiality).
8   Offer help but don't intrude.

The super eight

1 **Start small-scale and build on success**

2 **Clearly define the scheme's main purpose and scope**

3 **Influence the right people**

4 **Invest in training**

5 **Encourage effective matches**

6 **Monitor progress**

7 **Broadcast success (but preserve confidentiality)**

8 **Offer help but don't intrude**

III   The mentoring relationship

Introduction

In this section we examine the relationship between the mentee and mentor, almost like an outsider looking objectively to find out the essential qualities of an effective relationship. We also try to find a way of being able to learn from the successful ones and pass this learning on to others.

But what do you do if you're in the role of facilitator/administrator/champion and sense that things aren't working out too well between the mentor and mentee? Can you potentially learn more from failures than successes?

Effective mentoring relationships

If relationships aren't functioning well you won't have an effective scheme. There will be a lot of different interpretations of what works well and what doesn't but overall you will hope for far more successes than failures. Of course, you may be doing everything according to the book: clearly stated objectives well communicated, an apparently good matching process, training in line with needs, support in the right places – and yet somehow it's all 'only okay'. On the other hand, you may find really effective mentoring happening in the most unlikely places where you wouldn't think for one minute it would work. This apparent contradiction can be incredibly frustrating, particularly where you make strenuous efforts and yet success seems to pass you by. We won't dwell on this because we don't wish to encourage you to do all the apparent 'wrong things'. Let's examine what seems to constitute an effective relationship. We might simply say:

1   The mentee enjoys it and turns these good feelings into actions.
2   The mentor enjoys it, maybe has a new outlook on life in general and may also do something different as a result.

When we try to evaluate what people get out of mentoring we normally focus primarily on mentees. They in turn will usually talk about the behaviour of mentors. They will be described in this sort of way:

- listens to me
- asks really good questions
- is friendly and approachable
- avoids jumping to conclusions
- is non-judgemental
- can both give and receive constructive criticism
- gives me plenty of encouragement
- is open, honest and can be really trusted
- won't divulge our confidences to others.

You will be familiar with statements like these but what do you think about the following two situations?

After each session I go away thinking, 'How dare he say that to me?' and yet I go back for more. In similar vein, someone has described the feedback and information from mentoring as:

● What you least want to hear.
● What you most need to know.
● What you are least likely to be told.
● What you need the most help to deal with effectively.

There doesn't seem to be very much emphasis on empathy in these two examples! It is perhaps best seen, however, as 'horses for courses' and these statements are from examples of executive mentoring; as an executive you will have been confronted, challenged, faced some pretty harsh realities. If, on the other hand, you are working as a mentor of a young person who lacks confidence and has low self-esteem, while part of the process will probably involve challenge, it is perhaps best done in a less forthright and less brutal way than the examples quoted above. (Incidentally, this doesn't mean that many young people haven't also faced harsh realities.)

What we said above ((1) and (2)) we feel sums up effective mentoring relationships: positive feelings and outcomes.

What do we do about effective mentoring relationships?

First of all, if you are the facilitator/administrator it may be a case of leaving well alone – 'If it ain't broke don't fix it!' If you have a formal mentoring scheme you present participants with the rudiments of the process, hopefully give them some training and let them get on with it. If it's working well there's little point in interfering. You don't want to copy the behaviour of the exceptionally fastidious trainer who interferes to the extent that the trainees are meticulously informed of every single learning point that has been carefully written down in the training programme.

So how do you go about learning from these successful relationships?

No rocket science here but just think of the following process:

● What works well?
● What do we find difficult?
● What are the key learning features?

There are a number of ways in which you can arrive at the key learning features:

1 If you are a mentor as well as a facilitator think about your own mentoring experiences.
2 Have discussions with mentors and mentees on a one-to-one basis.
3 Arrange review meetings with all participants.
4 Obtain feedback from your mentoring support group (if you have one).

Whenever you are seeking feedback on mentoring it is important to discuss the process rather than facts and detailed discussion that has taken place between mentee and mentor. Preserving confidentiality is an integral part of effective mentoring.

As the facilitator, your aim will be to take note of the key learning features and incorporate these where possible to improve the overall effectiveness of your own scheme. It may be useful to involve the mentoring scheme's champion or sponsor in the discussion and review.

What do you do when you sense there are difficulties in relationships?

If you sense there are genuine difficulties you will almost certainly feel obliged to do something. While you may experience some discomfort about having to tackle situations like this, the positive aspect of this probably represents even greater learning opportunities than those arising from the more successful mentoring relationships. Having said all that, it is paramount that you tread very warily. It may simply be your perception that things aren't working too well in the relationship. If either party approaches you it's then apparent that some action is needed. We have suggested a process earlier in the manual under the sub-section, 'Influencing mentors and mentees' p. 81, which involves you asking the right sort of questions and listening very carefully· to the answers. See the mentor and mentee either separately or together to enable them to:

● review the difficulties objectively
● contract for new behaviour
● if appropriate, agree the mentoring relationship should come to an end
● end positively recalling some of the benefits.

To learn from some of the difficulties and adversities we suggest you go back to the Kolb Learning Cycle that was discussed in Chapter 1 (p. 8):

● Action
● Reflection
● Conclusion
● Planning

You will be able to *learn from mistakes and success*. Remember, effective mentoring is about *effective mentoring relationships*.

Chapter 4

Taking action

Assuming you have read Chapter 3 you may have already decided what you want to do next. You may have found some activities or forms that can be used to take you to the next stage; this could be planning the implementation of a scheme or a review of what you've got in place. Alternatively, our material may have triggered things you were going to do and you can adopt your own forms.

If you are proposing to do something different the process could look like this:

- This is where I am/we are now.
- This is where I think I/we need to be.
- This is what I propose to do.
- This is the sort of help I need.
- This is what I need to set up so that I can measure my/our success.

Of course, this is all very logical and if you have taken the trouble to read so far it makes sense to put something into practice. The exception could be if you used the manual to check out what you are currently doing and are satisfied with your current scheme.

If you acknowledge that there are things for you or your organization to do we suggest that you now need to avoid the 'good course' syndrome. By this we mean the situation where you or someone you know has been on a course, comes away with good intentions about action plans and 'commitment to personal change' and then does absolutely nothing different. The usual argument, and in many respects it is quite plausible, is: 'I might be prepared to change but I'm the only one who has been on the course and everything around me is just the same as always.'

If you have a pivotal role in mentoring we feel sure that you will want to get as far removed as possible from negative attitudes and will be thinking about two aspects of change:

1 What should I do differently or better?
2 What do I need to do to bring about change here?

Developing these a little further and based on the process referred to above you may wish to ask yourself the following questions:

- What will I do to set up mentoring in my organization?
- What will I do to evaluate our current scheme (if appropriate)?
- What will I do to influence others?
- What will I do to help develop mentoring skills in the organization?
- What will I do to develop my own skills as a mentor?

Action sheets

On the following pages (pp. 141–151) there are four action sheets for you to complete. Select the appropriate one for your particular situation. To help you, make use of the notes below, or refer back to relevant sections in the text.

Action sheet 1 – Guidance notes

Setting up mentoring

Where are we now?
Have there been any previous attempts at mentoring? Are any other current/previous initiatives relevant to a scheme? Include dates and any relevant information.

Where do we need to be?
Think of the sort of mentoring you are looking for. Will it be informal or formal? Would you start with a pilot scheme? Who would be involved as mentees and mentors? What would be the main objectives? Include dates and key stages if you feel you are able to include these now.

Who else needs to be involved?
Assuming you have the principal responsibility for setting up the scheme list names of others you will need to contact. This may be a case of enlisting the help of key people in the organization with power and influence. Consider involving others who may have prior knowledge and experience of mentoring. Test your ideas on others.

Actions to be taken and by whom
The key areas to consider here include clarification of objectives, the scope of the scheme, the matching process, how it will be publicized. Include dates and specify who is responsible for what.

Measuring progress
Include dates and action to review progress.

Influencing
See the forms on pp. 77–80.

ACTION SHEET 1 – SETTING UP MENTORING

Facilitator/administrator   Date

1   Where are we now?

2   Where do we need to be?

3   Who else needs to be involved

4   Actions to be taken and by whom

5   Measuring progress

Additional comments/possible constraints

Action sheet 2 – Guidance notes

Mentoring scheme evaluation

Where are we now?
A brief history of the scheme. Establish why it is appropriate to review the scheme at the current time. Include dates of any previous review and comments made at the time. Describe where the scheme appears to work well and where difficulties have been experienced.

Where do we need to be?
Refer to objectives, are these being met? Could much more be achieved? Is it a pilot scheme whose scope needs to be extended? Review the guidelines and re-write if appropriate with revised time-scales.

Who else needs to be involved?
As part of the review it would be useful to seek the views of mentees, mentors, line managers, the scheme's champion or sponsor.

Actions to be taken and by whom
Establish your review methods. Do you wish to arrange meetings, have informal discussion, and send out questionnaires?

Review targets with dates and amendment to current scheme
Confirmation of action taken. Write up notes and incorporate into a revised scheme outline or ground rules as appropriate. Include date when the scheme will be next subject to review.

ACTION SHEET 2 – MENTORING SCHEME EVALUATION

Facilitator/administrator   Date

1   Where are we now?

2   Where do we need to be?

3   Who else needs to be involved?
    (include names of mentees, mentors, line managers)

4   Actions to be taken and by whom

5   Revised targets with dates and written amendment

Additional comments

Action sheet 3 – Guidance notes

Developing mentoring skills

Where are we now?
You may be wishing to carry out a review either because you are seeking to improve the skills of your mentors or you are about to implement a scheme. In the case of the former you can identify needs through difficulties that may have been highlighted by mentors or mentees. Where you are putting in place a new scheme your training needs should be aligned with the scheme's main objectives and the capabilities of prospective mentors.

Where do we need to be?
Mentoring will be new to most people. Ideally you will want mentors who can quickly adapt to a role which may be somewhat different to what they've done before. Funding for training may be limited and, while ideally you would like each mentor to have two to three days training, you may have to settle for less or nothing at all. This could be a situation where you need to influence others to secure adequate funding.

Who else needs to be involved?
When your mentors have been chosen you can check whether or not they have had previous experience. You will need to decide how training needs can be met. It may be necessary to use an external provider.

Actions to be taken and by whom
Assuming you are the facilitator/administrator you will have the task of identifying needs and planning appropriate training programmes in line with the availability of mentors and the available budget.

Measuring progress
Set up the means to evaluate the training of mentors.

ACTION SHEET 3 – DEVELOPING MENTORING SKILLS

Facilitator/administrator   Date

1   Where are we now?

2   Where do we need to be?

3   Who else needs to be involved?

4   Actions to be taken and by whom
    (include strategy to secure funding for training)

5   Measuring progress

Additional comments/possible constraints

Action sheet 4 – Guidance notes

Developing my mentoring skills

Where am I now?
If you are a facilitator for a mentoring scheme you may already be quite familiar with the role of mentor. If not, reference to other parts of the manual particularly Section 3, 'Key Roles', should give you some appreciation of what is expected. It will be useful for you to think of previous learning experiences and to establish how you learn best. Is it through actual participation, reflecting or figuring out how things work? In the past, have you been helped by someone who might be classed as a mentor, whether this was on a formal or informal basis? What sort of skills do you currently have which would help you in the role of mentor?

Where do I need to be?
Having got a feel for the mentoring role and established your current skill level what are your training needs? What sort of targets do you need to set yourself to monitor your progress?

Who else needs to be involved?
Who else do you need to approach to give you feedback on your level of skill? Think of colleagues at work, partners and friends. Situations outside work and the way you do things could be directly relevant to your mentoring role.

Actions to be taken by you
This can be a summary of the outcomes from the previous three questions. You are going through the process of understanding the role, some self-analysis and establishing needs. If your organization is currently setting up a mentoring scheme you are likely to be part of a training development programme for all mentors. But if the scheme is already established you may have to request training to meet your specific needs.

Measuring progress
Establish targets to monitor your progress with a time-scale. Establish how you will contract with your mentee to give you feedback at various stages in your relationship.

ACTION SHEET 4 – DEVELOPING MY MENTORING SKILLS

Name   Date

1   Where am I now?

2   Where do I need to be?

3   Who else needs to be involved?
    (feedback from others)

Reproduced from *The Mentoring Manual* by Mike Whittaker and Ann Cartwright,
Gower, Aldershot

4   Actions to be taken by me

5   Measuring progress

Additional comments/possible difficulties

Actions for mentees, mentors and champions

We hope that there is something in this book for you, whatever role you have in mentoring. It is of course quite possible that you have all sorts of involvement in your own scheme. In the following section we suggest you review your role with a view to considering changes that will be of benefit to you.

Mentees

Do you remember our summary of successful learning in the Introduction? This was adapted from Kolb's Learning Cycle model (see p. 8).

If you take your current mentoring relationship, what are your feelings about it? You and your mentor may have worked together for some considerable time and the relationship seems to be very productive for both of you. Do you want more from it? On the other hand, perhaps it's a bit problematic and you wonder if you are suited to each other. In either situation take some time out and work through the following:

- What am I getting from the relationship?
- What seems to work well?
- What is difficult?
- What would I like my mentor to do differently?
- What could I do differently?
- What will I do differently?

If you have access to our previous book, *32 Activities on Coaching and Mentoring*, (Gower, 1997) there are several review activities you could use. You might want to try, 'Mentoring – progress review', for instance.

Something else you might wish to consider if you have had the experience of being a mentee is to try your hand at becoming a mentor. As we stated at the beginning of the manual, benefits from mentoring can accrue also to mentors. Mentees usually make good mentors. If your organization has a formal mentoring scheme why not seek opportunities to become a mentor? You may also find opportunities outside work.

Mentors

Similar to the mentee, the suggestion is that you spend some time reviewing the effectiveness of your mentoring relationship. It is important to avoid any complacency and to seek areas for improvement.

- How well do we work together?
- What have we achieved?

- What has been difficult?
- What might we do differently?
- How might I suggest that we do things in a different way?
- What changes will we actually make?

Think of your own performance as a mentor.

- Identify your particular strengths
- Identify areas you need to work on
- Establish how you would do this
- What additional training would be helpful to you?
- What will you agree to do to improve your effectiveness as a mentor?

Do you pass on your learning experiences to others?

- Have you got a mentoring support group?
- How effective is it?
- What could you do to make it more effective?
- Do you give positive messages to others about the benefits of mentoring?
- Could you do more?
- What will you agree to do now to add to the effectiveness of mentoring?

What about your own future?

- Since you became a mentor have you taken stock of the skills you have been using?
- Could you now make better use of these skills?
- Has your outlook changed?
- Do you wish to make changes in your life?
- What do you intend to do?

Write down the most significant thing you have gained from mentoring and the most important piece of learning for you.

Champions

You probably hate the word 'champion' and feel it does not apply to you. On the other hand, behind every successful scheme there is likely to be one person who, as a prime source of encouragement and influence, can make or break a scheme. For some people, mentoring is a new concept which sits uneasily with other more tangible things such as making a profit, reaching targets, getting results and answering to others. Some source of inspiration is needed to provide a balance between the 'hard' facts and the 'softer' issues.

So what about your scheme?

- Does it work as well as you would like it to?

- What have been the main successes?
- Has it failed in any area?
- Do you know people for whom it has not worked?
- What changes do you think are needed?
- What will you do to effect these changes?

What about your own role and influence?

- Have you devoted as much time to mentoring as you would like?
- Has mentoring at times taken second place to other issues?
- Do you feel okay about this?
- Where have you been particularly successful in influencing others?
- Where have you been less successful?
- What might you do about this?
- What will you agree to do differently?

What about the future of mentoring?

- Is it here to stay in your organization?
- If it has a limited life why is this?
- Does it need to be extended to other areas?
- What will you need to do to make this happen?

Confirming the benefits of mentoring

- Write down the main personal benefit you have experienced from mentoring.
- Write down the main benefit to the organization.

Are these what you expected when mentoring was envisaged?

Chapter 5

Developing mentoring skills

Introduction

In earlier chapters we have considered the part training will play in getting mentoring into place. 'Training considerations' in Chapter 3 posed questions about the place of training in mentoring and hopefully provided the reader with some ideas and answers. In Chapter 4 the Action Sheet, 'Developing mentoring skills', presented the reader with a basic format for reviewing needs and taking action based on these needs. In this chapter, the four sections provide the reader with additional guidance. Reference is again made to *32 Activities on Coaching and Mentoring*.

The four sections are:

1   Sample activities and how they might be used
2   An outline of the remaining activities
3   Example of a mentoring workshop
4   Guidance notes for mentors.

In this list, the sample 'activities' in a streamline version are: 'Using intuition as an aid to mentoring' (M6), 'Using my experience to help you' (M7), 'Acknowledging the stages of development' (M11). Section (2) consists of an outline of the remaining mentoring 'activities' with a brief description and situations where they could be used. There are four self-assessment and 20 other activities. Section (3) refers to details of a workshop which we ran looking at the process from original design through to implementation. Section (4) refers to handouts which have been used as back-up material on workshops run by one of the writers. A 'Mentoring Agreement' is included which facilitators can adapt for their own scheme. The material could be used as a handout if appropriate.

1   Sample activities and how they might be used

The following is a suggestion of the way the three sample 'activities' could be incorporated into a mentoring workshop or into the mentoring review process.

1   **M6   'Using intuition as an aid to mentoring'**
    M7   'Using my experience to help you'

Earlier in the manual we said that the traditional 'show and tell' style of training is likely to be inappropriate in developing mentoring skills. Delegates need to practise the sort of skills they will subsequently use in the role of mentor and to receive feedback on what they have done. These two 'activities' could be used on a workshop as follows:

- introductions and objectives
- mentoring – uses and benefits
- identifying the main skills involved
- using intuition as an aid to mentoring – practice and feedback
- details of the organization's mentoring scheme
- using my experience to help you – practice and feedback
- key learning points
- agreed actions.

2   **M11   'Acknowledging the stages of development'**

This activity could be used on a follow-up workshop where delegates already have some experience of mentoring and they are already beginning to identify the various phases of mentoring. It will be appropriate to share mutual experiences on the workshop.

If your organization has a support group or carries out periodic reviews on a fairly formal basis, this could be seen as a potential learning situation with this particular activity incorporated into the review process.

M6   'Using intuition as an aid to mentoring'

Description

The *Concise Oxford Dictionary* defines intuition as: 'Immediate apprehension without the intervention of any reasoning process.' This activity enables mentors to explore their current intuitive skills, consider how they might be improved and how they might contribute to the mentoring relationship.

Situation

This activity is appropriate where the mentoring relationship could benefit from a fresh approach or level to provide new ideas and directions. Instinctive feelings about someone else's thoughts and emotions, when proved to be accurate, provide the mentee with psychological support from a 'skilled' partner.

Aims

- to assess the mentor's intuitive skills
- to help develop these skills
- to put improved intuitive skills into practice
- to appreciate the enjoyment and benefits derived from intuition.

Method

1   Reflect on intuitive skills (by the mentor)
Think of situations where your intuitive skills have proved to be extremely accurate. You may wish to select examples from your childhood. Write down some key words and pick several intuitive skills which you might use in your mentoring relationship. Focus on images, flashes of inspiration and hunches.

2   Experiment
Try out these skills in different situations, including your next mentoring session.

3   Review
How did your intuitive skills work out in these situations? Include feedback from others in your review. What did you do well? What would you like to use again? What proved to be difficult?

4   Continuing your development
Create situations which help to develop these skills. For example, take a back seat in a meeting and *listen*, *observe*, *interpret*.

Then after the meeting, *check*: 'At the meeting, although you said ..., it seemed to me you were actually feeling ...'

Timing

This exercise could be confined to a few minutes of useful reflection or you may wish to develop your intuitive skills over a considerable period of time.

M7   'Using my experience to help you'

Description

This activity enables the mentors to reflect on past experiences and mentees to draw on the knowledge and experience. The process involves asking questions rather than 'telling'.

Situation

This is best suited to a well-developed and trusting mentoring relationship.

Aims

- to review significant events and learning experiences (the mentor)
- to identify information that could be of help to the mentee
- to encourage the mentee to ask probing questions
- to encourage the mentee to consider making changes, whether or not these are as a direct result of this discussion.

Method

1   The mentor reviews his/her own life to date, selecting key events, high points, low points and significant learning experiences.

- my childhood
- growing up
- my education
- my relationships
- my family
- my career
- my interests
- my beliefs
- my future.

The mentor will have to carefully consider the extent of self-disclosure; too much and the emotional effects could overwhelm both or either party. In a well-established relationship the mentor should be in a position to get the balance about right. This review is best carried out prior to the mentoring session and taking notes may be helpful.

2   At the session itself it would be useful to agree a contract between the parties covering these sort of areas:

- encouraging questions from the mentee rather than 'telling'

- acknowledging differences between the two parties
- examining similarities/differences
- pausing to identify examples which seem particularly valuable
- requesting feedback from the mentee
- identifying actions the mentee may wish to take as a result of the activity
- exchanging feelings about the process.

3 Encourage the mentee to ask open question about the mentor's experiences.
4 Review the process, feelings and agreed actions.

Timing

The activity would normally last the length of one mentoring session. If the process is of particular appeal to both parties it could be adopted for future meetings.

M11 'Acknowledging the stages of development'

This 'activity' could be used on a follow-up workshop where delegates already have some experience of mentoring and they are beginning to identify the various phases of mentoring. It will be appropriate to share mutual experiences on the workshop.

If your organization has a support group or carries out periodic review on a fairly formal basis this could be seen as a potential learning situation with this particular activity incorporated into the review process.

Description

This activity presents a model of mentoring with four stages and enables partners to establish their current position. This one to one exercise involving the mentee and mentor is best used in a fairly well-established relationship (see the OHP transparency copy on p. 161).

Situations

Even if the mentoring relationship is working well either or both parties may feel they would like to review the stage they have reached. If, however, some difficulties are being experienced this activity can provide the impetus to move on.

Aims

- to enable partners to identify the stage they have reached in their relationship and decide how they might move on

- to contribute to the mentoring relationship
- to review learning and benefits experienced by both parties
- to gain personal insights.

Method

The review process uses a four-stage model with a career analogy:

Mentoring relationship	*Career*
• first meeting	new job – first day
• beginning to understand	two months in the job
• learning and incorporating change	two years in the job
• completing.	moving on.

1   Either party may suggest it would be beneficial to review the relationship.

2   Consider the model that emphasizes the emotional experiences throughout the relationship and use the career analogy if this seems appropriate.

3   Establish the stage reached and feelings about this (could be between stages).

4   Talk through benefits, actions taken and difficulties experienced.

5   Establish what stage you will reach next. The model suggests incremental rather than dramatic and sudden change. If problems are highlighted this is an opportune time to discuss them.

6   If you feel you are moving towards the next stage it will be helpful to agree appropriate actions as you advance towards this transition. This is particularly important if you are moving towards 'Completion'. A contract at this stage to finish at an agreed date in the future is likely to cause less pain than a sudden termination.

Timing

This activity is likely to take up one mentoring session.

Mentoring four-stage model

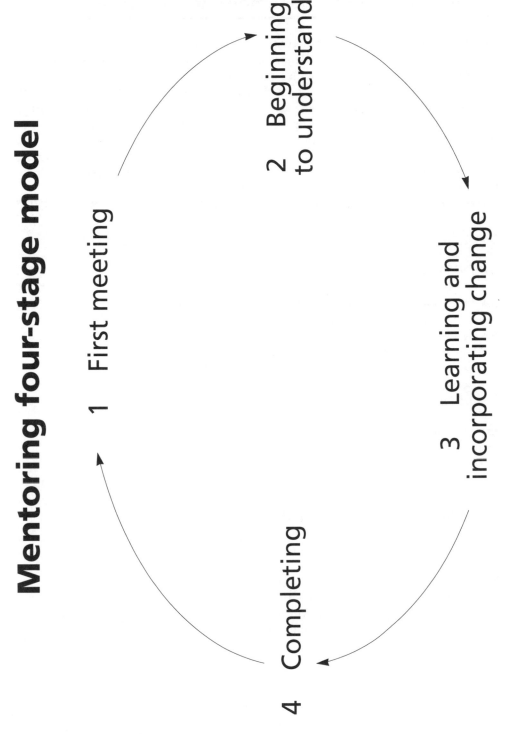

1 First meeting

2 Beginning to understand

3 Learning and incorporating change

4 Completing

Reproduced from *The Mentoring Manual* by Mike Whittaker and Ann Cartwright, Gower, Aldershot

2   An outline of the remaining 'activities'

The outlines of the remaining activities are classified on an ascending scale in terms of the development of a mentor. They start with self-assessment, even posing the question as to whether someone wants to become a mentor and progress to the final stages of a mentoring relationship and how to deal with endings. They are called 'outlines' and should give you a feel for the sort of issues that arise in developing mentoring skills. You may then wish to explore these in more detail and refer to our previous manual, *32 Activities on Coaching and Mentoring* (Gower, 1997). These activities may be purchased as a collection under the title referred to. Alternatively, you can purchase them *individually* through the Gower training website <www.gowertraining.co.uk>.

A summary of the outlines are now listed, followed by more detailed descriptions.

Self-assessment

SA1   Significant learning experiences
SA2   Do I want to be a mentor?
SA3   Mentoring – a skills clinic
SA4   Assessing my mentoring style

Beginning the process

M1   Building the mentoring relationship
M2   Rediscovering curiosity
M3   Understanding organizational culture

Building a range of mentoring skills

M4   Acting as a sounding board
M5   Being honest
M6   Using intuition as an aid to mentoring
M7   Using my experience to help you
M8   Learning to view the world from someone else's 'hilltop'
M9   Radiant thinking and mind mapping

Reviewing and revising progress

M10   Mentoring – progress review
M11   Acknowledging the stages of development
M12   Developing support groups
M13   Measuring success
M14   Overcoming difficulties arising from others' perceptions
M15   Mentors can 'put their foot in it'
M16   Learning to let go

Putting the skills to different uses

M17   Changing direction
M18   Reversing roles
M19   Developing a co-mentoring relationship
M20   Developing strategic awareness

SA1   Significant learning experiences

Description

This activity is designed to help you to reflect on your past experiences and give you some insight into how you learnt and developed the skills and abilities you have now. As a mentor you can then get others to reflect on their learning experiences in a similar way. Even if their preferences are different to yours, this knowledge will assist the mentoring process.

Situations

You may wish to use an activity like this when you start off as a mentor or come back to it whenever it feels appropriate. It can also usefully be incorporated into a workshop.

SA2   Do I want to be a mentor?

Description

This is your own guided tour around learning experiences at significant times in your life, how you have been helped and some conclusions to enable you to decide whether or not you wish to become a mentor. Key events in your life can be linked to such themes as:

- childhood
- adolescence
- education
- work
- relationships
- life and death.

Situations

Perhaps your organization is requesting volunteers to become mentors. Alternatively, you may have been thinking about mentoring for some time, possibly triggered by a cry for help from a friend or colleague, and asked yourself, 'Is this for me?'

SA3   Mentoring – a skills clinic

Description

This activity is centred on a questionnaire that helps mentors assess their skill levels. By obtaining feedback from mentees and colleagues, mentors can then develop their own action plans. Mentors rate their own performance on seven skill areas on a 1–5 scale with 1 indicating exceptional ability. The skill areas are:

- questioning
- listening
- summarizing
- giving feedback
- influencing
- counselling
- coaching.

Situations

This activity can be used as part of a development programme for mentors. Alternatively, it could be in response to situations such as:

- The mentor needs feedback on his/her progress as a mentor.
- A difficult situation arose and there was disappointment in the way it was resolved.
- A perceived need to improve the mentoring relationship.

SA4   *Assessing my mentoring style*

Description

In this activity mentors assess their mentoring style by selecting three situations where they 'helped' another person and then identifying which helping style they adopted (see OHP transparency copy on p. 166). These are classed as:

- telling
- advising
- manipulating
- counselling.

Feedback is then obtained from a colleague or partner to establish the appropriateness of the style adopted for each particular situation. This enables the mentor to agree changes in style if needed.

Situations

This can be used individually or as part of a development workshop.

Basic helping styles

Excludes mentee

Telling   **Manipulating**

**Problem
Centred**   **Mentee
Centred**

Advising   **Counselling**

Includes mentee

Reproduced from *The Mentoring Manual* by Mike Whittaker and Ann Cartwright,
Gower, Aldershot

M1   Building the mentoring relationship

Description

This activity is designed to help both the mentor and mentee to begin to develop a deeper insight and understanding of each other's views and values. It involves use of a workbook containing a number of discussion statements. The activity encourages unconditional listening and is designed to begin the process of building a supportive relationship.

Situations

This activity can be used at the start of a relationship or at various stages during it. It could be helpful if there has been some confusion or misunderstanding.

M2   Rediscovering curiosity

Description

This activity is designed to encourage and enable participants to rediscover the art of being curious that many of us, sadly, leave behind in childhood. Rediscovering curiosity helps to develop more enquiring and challenging approaches to life and to face life's challenges and changes as new adventures. After an examination of the various definitions of curiosity, the activity provides a number of exercises to encourage novel and lateral thinking.

Situations

This is suitable for any situation where there is a need for participants to question and challenge their perceptions of the world around them. It can be used as a one to one exercise or as part of a development programme for mentors.

M4   Acting as a sounding board

Description

This activity is designed normally to be used by pairs. It enables one partner to 'act as a sounding board' for the other. It provides the first partner with the opportunity to think aloud any thoughts, ideas or plans they might have. Alternatively, as part of a development workshop, by operating in trios the roles of speaker, listener and observer can be rotated to provide the opportunity for detailed feedback.

Situations

This activity can be used when the first partner wants/needs to:

- talk through their thoughts, ideas, or plans before implementing them
- prepare themselves for a difficult/stressful situation
- practise selling an idea to another person.

M5   Being honest

Description

This activity is designed to encourage openness and honesty between people, however painful or difficult it may be. To help the process use is made of a questionnaire to be completed by the mentee under the guidance of the mentor. The area of concern or conflict is identified. Feelings are explored in depth as are the range of options facing the mentee.

Situation

It can be used to:

- provide open and honest feedback
- identify and prompt discussion about areas of concern or conflict.

(M6 and M7 described earlier, pp. 156–159.)

M8   Learning to view the world from someone else's 'hilltop'

Description

The 'hilltop' concept suggests that because of various factors such as background, education, hopes, fears, ambitions, etc., we all have our own unique perspective of the world. This activity is designed to encourage empathy with and understanding of other people, their views, values and opinions.

Situations

This activity can be used to develop and increase the level of empathy and understanding within a mentoring relationship. It can also be used as part of a development workshop to help people to recognize and value the differences between them.

M9   Radiant thinking and mind mapping

Description

This activity introduces participants to the concepts of radiant thinking and mind mapping. The creative skills practised can subsequently be used to enhance outcomes and actions from the mentoring relationship, particularly when new initiatives are being sought. There are similarities here with 'rediscovering curiosity' in that the process can involve some unlearning and getting away from long-accepted approaches based purely on logic.

Situations

- as part of a workshop for developing mentors and mentees
- as an input to a meeting of a mentoring support group (if you have one)
- as help in providing a solution to a problem or suggesting a new direction in the search for a solution.

M10   Mentoring – progress review

Description

This activity focuses on an individual mentoring relationship and encourages both mentor and mentee to agree a format for reviewing the progress of the actions taken by the mentee. Both may or may not choose to make use of an accompanying progress review sheet.

Situations

This activity is likely to be particularly appropriate during the early stages of the mentoring relationship, when both parties may experience some uncertainty and apprehension. Questions such as the following may arise:

- What is the real significance of mentoring?
- What do we hope to achieve?
- How can we measure progress?

This activity encourages mentor and mentee to establish a simple, uncomplicated method for reviewing actions taken by the mentee.

(M11 described earlier, pp. 159–160.)

M12   Developing support groups

Description

In this activity mentees examine the support they currently have and the type of support they need. Ways of obtaining support are explored with the help of the mentor. An action plan format is also included if both parties feel this will be of help.

Situations

This activity can be used as part of a development workshop or within a mentoring session.

M13   Measuring success

Description

This differs from M10 'Mentoring – progress review' in that the focus here is primarily on a review of mentoring in the organization rather than on individual mentoring relationships. The activity will enable facilitators/administrators/ champions of mentoring to review success within their organization. If needed, however, mentors or mentees could extract relevant sections to monitor their own progress. The following nine criteria can be used as a measure of the success of a mentoring scheme:

1   Meetings – do they take place as planned?
2   Objectives – are they both agreed and flexible?
3   Expectations in the mentoring relationship – are these met even if they may change?
4   Stages of mentoring relationship – is there an awareness of these?
5   Actions – is the mentee actually doing something different in line with what he/she agreed?
6   Benefits – for both mentee and mentor?
7   Behaviour – is there mutual respect and trust?
8   Progress review of the relationship – does this happen?
9   Confidentiality – is this always maintained?

Situations

Mentoring is likely to have been in place for some time, is enjoying some success and the facilitator may wish to identify the critical success factors to lead to even greater improvement.

M15   Mentors can 'put their foot in it'

Description

This is an activity which confirms that all mentors are human and make mistakes. Fairly provocative statements are included to lure the mentor away from a false sense of security. If the mentor is insensitive to some sort of clumsy behaviour which has had a negative effect on the mentee, the latter might very well want the mentor to read through this activity.

Situations

The reason to use this could arise from the perception of either mentor or mentee. It could be used on a development programme to remind mentors to avoid complacency.

M16   Learning to let go

Description

This activity is designed to help the mentor to 'end' the mentoring relationship at the appropriate time and to help both parties recognize that as well as being a sad time it can also be a time to celebrate. Three ending strategies are considered:

1 Fixed-term contract
2 The weaning process
3 The review process.

Situations

This activity can be used to bring the mentoring relationship to a satisfactory conclusion. It can also be used as part of a development workshop.

M17   Changing direction

Description

The activity encourages the mentee to identify situations which they would like to change. It is a process which encourages careful reflection rather than providing instant solutions. If the mentor senses a feeling of powerlessness on behalf of the mentee use can be made of the four options in the 'Options for Change' model as follows:

1   Stay with it and stop moaning.
2   Work for change in others and/or the system.
3   Get out.
4   Work for change in self.

Situations

The initiative for this activity can come from the mentor or the mentee. There may well be a background of frustration at the lack or pace of change.

M18   Reversing roles

Description

As the relationship develops there will be times when the mentor will appreciate the benefits the mentee has brought, and times when support, ideas and guidance can be reciprocated. This activity involves role reversal to cover a specific situation rather than simply exchanging roles long term.

Situations

● The mentor wishes to share a problem/situation with the mentee.
● The mentee perceives that help/guidance is required.
● Both parties feel it is appropriate to reverse roles for a given situation.
● At some future date the mentee may wish to become a mentor (not to be used as a role play; use real issues).

M19   Developing a co-mentoring relationship

Description

In this activity people are encouraged to develop a co-mentoring relationship over a period of time. As part of the process, each person gives the other unconditional time and space during initial brief five-minute meetings and then building gradually towards 30-minute sessions. The activity demonstrates that people outside the formal organization, who may not be considered wiser or more experienced, can use the mentoring process.

Situations

The following people can use the activity:

- at the same level within the organization
- in the same profession but from different organizations
- working in isolation, for example consultants, chief executives, self-employed professionals, etc.
- as part of their own continuing professional development.

M20   Developing strategic awareness

Description

This activity is designed to encourage participants to broaden their perspectives and to develop more effective medium- and long-term plans for themselves and the organizations they work for. It involves an examination of three stages in the *strategic management process*:

1 Strategic analysis
2 Strategic choice
3 Strategic implementation.

Situations

The activity is suitable for any situations involving the planning of future activities or goals. It is also suitable for any one seeking to develop the ability to look at the 'wider picture'.

3   Example of a mentoring workshop

Introduction

This is a brief description and evaluation of a workshop designed and run by the writer in November 1998. At the end of the section there is an outline of the full programme, which was entitled 'Mentoring and Peer Mentoring'. It was aimed predominantly at delegates who were in professions associated with young people, for example teachers and social workers.

Designing the workshop

With an 'open' programme like this it is quite difficult to anticipate needs. You design an event that you hope will be both of interest and benefit to those people who are attending. There are fundamental considerations such as:

- Is this about mentoring for themselves or for the people they are working with?
- How much mentoring is already taking place within their organizations?
- How much mentoring experience do they have?
- Should the emphasis be on mentoring or peer mentoring?

As part of the design process the writer finds it useful to put himself in the shoes of delegates and to think, 'What might I be looking for in a programme like this?' In this particular case the list was:

- I need to develop/improve my mentoring skills.
- I want to know more about mentoring.
- What's the big deal about mentoring?
- I feel uncomfortable about mentoring. What can help?
- What are the main mentoring skills?
- Do you need special qualities to be a mentor?
- What's it actually like to be mentored?
- My boss has asked me to find out all I can about mentoring.
- What are the latest developments in mentoring?
- How do I set up an effective mentoring scheme?
- How do I run mentoring training effectively?
- How might I improve our existing scheme?
- What are the benefits of peer mentoring?
- Can you be both mentor and line manager to the same person?

A list like this is quite daunting but it is a useful starting point. The aim was to provide delegates with a practical event conducted in a relaxed atmosphere. Having considered needs the objectives were presented as:

- to have examined mentoring in action
- to have practised mentoring skills
- to have reviewed delegates' mentoring schemes
- to have agreed actions on personal skills development/delegates' mentoring schemes.

These were tested during the introduction and appeared to be about in line with expectations.

The proposed workshop outline was:

1   starting off
2   mentoring definitions and mentoring in practice
3   reviewing delegates' experiences
4   mentoring skills – review and practice
5   effective mentoring – a blueprint for success
6   peer mentoring
7   agreed actions
8   workshop review.

How did things work out?

The interesting aspect of training events is that things often do not work out as planned. It is worth planning for the unexpected. As a result of an accident on The Queensway in the centre of Birmingham the programme started more than half an hour late. There were fewer delegates than expected. The levels of previous exposure to mentoring varied enormously. It was very interesting to note that with peer mentoring there seemed to be as much experience of pupil-to-pupil mentoring as adult-to-adult.

The areas in the programme outline described at the end of this section (pp. 177–180) were covered but not necessarily in the same order nor with the degree of emphasis originally planned. Where it was originally intended to look at everybody's mentoring scheme in their own organization in some depth towards the latter stages of the workshop, delegates divided into two working groups to focus on the implementation of mentoring in just two of the delegates' schemes. This made practical sense as the majority of delegates came from organizations where no mentoring scheme was in place.

Below, the writer reviews what went well and what could have been done differently.

Evaluation

The feedback was mostly positive and delegates appeared to have both enjoyed the workshop and found it to be of practical use.

The positives

- The practical sessions where delegates worked in pairs to assess and develop their mentoring skills worked well (allowing for time constraints). These were based on two activities in *32 Activities on Coaching and Mentoring* (Gower, 1997), 'Mentoring a Skills Clinic' (SA3) and 'Building the Mentoring Relationship' (M1).
- Quoting from mentoring schemes (researched for this book) gave delegates an up to date review of some examples of mentoring schemes in action.
- Guidelines on what constitutes effective mentoring provided a useful backcloth to delegates' existing or projected mentoring schemes.
- The practical work in two groups on two delegates' mentoring schemes led to excellent co-operation and two effective presentations.

Areas for improvement

- More information prior to the workshop on delegates' needs would have made course design that much easier.
- Less discussion in the plenary group and more pairs or group work.
- Several delegates would have liked additional information on mentoring in other sectors such as manufacturing.

On pages 177–180 is a form showing a mentoring workshop outline, followed by OHP transparency copies for use with it.

MENTORING WORKSHOP OUTLINE

1 Starting off

Welcome and domestics

Objectives:

- mentoring in action
- mentoring skills   **OHP**
- review of your existing/new schemes
- action points.

Ground rules: 'What do we need to do to make this event a success?'
          (2 groups)

Methods: Informal, working together, practical, pairs, groups

Introductions

- Name
- Job
- Your mentoring experience   **Flip chart**
- Two things you want from this workshop

2 Mentoring – definitions and practice

What do you understand by the word 'mentoring'?   **Flip chart**

Mentoring definitions   **OHP**

> 'Providing guidance, support and practical help through life crises or transitions or into new stages of development.'

> 'So they can stand alone.'

Also, 'For Cynics Only'   **OHP**

'Why has mentoring become so fashionable?'   **Plenary group**

'What are the potential benefits from mentoring?'

- to the organization

Reproduced from *The Mentoring Manual* by Mike Whittaker and Ann Cartwright,   *177*
Gower, Aldershot

- to the mentor **Two groups**
- to the mentee.

Discussion in plenary group

The overuse/misuse of the word 'mentoring'
Examples of mentoring in practice:

1   to encourage equality for:
    - ethnic minorities
    - disabled people
    - women aiming for management (in male-dominated cultures).
2   as part of development programmes for graduates
3   support to start new businesses
4   continuing professional development
5   support for young offenders (e.g. BEAT project in West Midlands)
6   executive mentoring.

3   Looking at our experiences

Experience of delegates' own schemes **Pairs**

- Who's involved?
- What are the objectives?
- What works well?
- What's been difficult?

Share in plenary group **Plenary**

Tutor's own research on mentoring schemes

What constitutes an effective scheme? **Discussion**

Ground rules for effective mentoring **OHP**

4   Mentoring skills – review and practice

What are the main mentoring skills? **Discussion**

Start of skills development

Process:

- What am I like as a mentor?
- skills practice

● reflections.

Use of 'Mentoring a Skills Clinic' (SA3) (from *32 Activities on Coaching and Mentoring*) **Pairs**

Discussion in main group

'Building the mentoring relationship' (M1) (from *32 Activities on Coaching and Mentoring*) **Pairs**

Discussion in main group

Refer back to individual assessment under first execise above

What changes would you like to make?

5 Peer mentoring

Share experiences in main group **Group discussion**

What are the benefits?

What are main differences from the traditional concept of mentoring?

What actions might you take to set up/improve a peer mentoring relationship?

6 Mentoring schemes – a blueprint for success

Either design a new mentoring scheme or measure the success of one of the delegate's schemes using the following for guidance.

● scope
● objectives
● selection of mentors and mentees **Two groups**
● how to gain support
● training arrangements
● review mechanism.

Presentations and discussion in main group

Comparison with delegates' schemes (if appropriate)

7   Agreed actions

- your own mentoring scheme
- getting mentoring into place in your organization (if currently without a scheme)
- how you will improve your mentoring skills.

8   Workshop review

Objectives

○ Examined mentoring in action

○ Practised mentoring skills

○ Reviewed your scheme (if appropriate)

○ Agreed actions on skills/your scheme

Mentoring definitions

'Providing guidance, support and practical help through life crises or into new stages of development.'

'So they can stand alone.'

Reproduced from *The Mentoring Manual* by Mike Whittaker and Ann Cartwright, Gower, Aldershot

For cynics only

- Least want to hear

- Most need to know

- You are least likely to be told

- Need the most help to deal with effectively

4   Guidance notes for mentors

- Description of the mentoring process
- The skills and qualities needed by the mentor
- Outline for mentoring sessions
- Ground rules for the mentoring process
- Mentoring scheme agreement form

Description of the mentoring process

What is mentoring?

- The aim of the mentoring process is to provide both the mentor and the mentee with a cost-effective process of development that both meets their needs and fits into their time constraints.

- Mentoring is a relationship between two people in which trust and respect enables problems and difficulties to be discussed in an open and supportive environment. By sharing their experiences, issues and concerns within an open and trusting environment, each mentee is able to develop and grow and so maximize their respective potential.

- Mentoring is *not* about two people having a conversation. It is a structured process that gives the mentee an agreed period of 'unconditional time and space' to talk through issues, ideas and situations that are unique to them.

- Mentoring is an opportunity to use someone as a 'sounding board' for new ideas and initiatives. It also provides an opportunity for constructive reflection with someone who will be open and honest with you.

- Mentoring is an effective development tool for busy people.

The skills and qualities needed by the mentor

To be effective, mentors need to possess and/or develop the following skills and abilities:

- The ability to *listen and hear what is said.*
- The ability to *question and challenge* their own thinking and the thinking of others.
- The ability to *summarize and reflect back.*
- The ability to *give and receive constructive feedback.*
- The ability to *point out connections and contradictions.*
- The ability to display *empathy and understanding.*

- The ability to *encourage problem-solving and seek solutions.*
- The ability to *recognize and acknowledge emotions.*
- The ability to *trust others and be trusted by others.*
- The ability to be *open and honest with self and others.*
- The ability to be a *'tough friend'.*
- The ability to *give* as well as *receive* unconditional time and space.

Outline for mentoring sessions

1   Agree a mutually acceptable meeting place. If using either person's office remember to ensure that you are not disturbed.
2   Agree an end time and stick to it as far as possible. Try to allow for some time to review the process on an ongoing basis.
3   Prior to starting each new session it may be helpful for the mentee to take about five minutes to share and reflect on events that have occurred since the last meeting if they are not to be the main topic of discussion during the present session.
4   Prior to starting the period of unconditional time and space, the mentee should, if appropriate, identify any issues or areas that they would like the mentor to focus on and/or provide feedback on.
5   Unless the mentee specifically asks for advice and guidance about a particular problem, the mentor should not offer advice or solutions. Where solutions are sought, the mentor should try to adopt a problem-solving approach, i.e. to encourage the mentee to:

- identify the problem clearly and concisely
- explore the pros and cons of all possible solutions
- decide on the best course of action for the mentee at this time.

6   The mentor should challenge the mentee if they are continuously avoiding potential solutions, e.g. by adopting a 'yes but' approach.
7   Summarize and record if necessary all progress, decisions and agreed actions.
8   At the end of the periods of unconditional time and space it may be necessary to take a few minutes to refocus mentee's attention back to what they will be doing after the session. This is especially important if the session was very emotional or difficult for the mentee.
9   Arrange the date and time of the next meeting and any actions that will be taken by that date if appropriate.

Ground rules for the mentoring process

Confidentiality

- To be successful a mentoring relationship has to be built on trust and confidentiality is a key part of trust within any relationship.
- From the beginning, it is important that both mentor and the mentee have a shared understanding about what they want and what they expect from the relationship especially around issues of confidentiality.
- It may be helpful to spend the first session exploring this issue and agreeing a framework for future sessions.

Frequency, time-span and format of sessions

- It is up to both mentor and the mentee to agree the frequency, time-span and format of the sessions.
- However, it is recommended that sessions should be held at least monthly and last for at least one hour.
- Mentors and mentees can choose to meet more or less frequently, for shorter or longer periods.
- The important element is that the mentee feels that they are being given an agreed period of unconditional time and space.
- It is advisable to agree in advance as many dates and times of sessions as possible and to give each other a commitment that these dates and times will only be changed in an emergency.

Contents, behaviours and boundaries

- The mentor and the mentee needs to make it clear to the other if there are any issues they do not wish to discuss. For example:
  - some people are happier than others to discuss personal issues that may impact on their work
  - some people are also happier with sharing emotions or being touched than others are
  - some people are more willing to be supportively challenged than others are.
- At the beginning of the relationship it is important that the mentor and the mentee take the time to identify and share any boundaries or barriers.
- As the trust develops within the relationship, these boundaries and barriers may change.

Phone contact between sessions

- Both the mentor and the mentee need to agree beforehand if they are willing and able to provide telephone support between sessions.
- Whatever is agreed should be recorded and can be reviewed and changed as necessary.

Reviewing the co-mentoring partnership

- It is useful to build in regular review times to ensure that the mentoring relationship is still meeting the needs of both the mentor and the mentee and is working effectively.
- Reviews can be carried out at the end of each session or at agreed intervals.
- However, it is recommended that a review be carried out at least every 3–4 months.

MENTORING AGREEMENT FORM

This is a Mentoring Scheme Agreement between:

(Name)

and

(Name)

In signing this agreement, both partners agree the following:

- to meet for at least one hour every month for the next six months

- to keep all agreed mentoring appointments and/or to rearrange alternative appointment within five working days

- within that time, to give an agreed amount of unconditional time and space

- to carry out at least one review meeting during the six-month period

- to keep the content of the discussions confidential

- after the initial six-month period, to carry on with the mentoring relationship for as long as it continues to meet the needs of both the mentor and the mentee

- (optional, please delete if not appropriate) to provide telephone/fax/e-mail support to each other between mentoring sessions as needed.

Signed:

Date:

Signed:

Date:

Reproduced from *The Mentoring Manual* by Mike Whittaker and Ann Cartwright, Gower, Aldershot

Chapter 6

Writers' personal reflections

Personal reflections 1

These are some notes relating to my mentoring experiences over recent months. I have added anything I thought was relevant up to the date that we completed writing the book.

Birmingham, 4 November 1998

I ran this workshop on 'Mentoring and Peer Mentoring' for a group of nine people who were mainly teachers or had some connection with the development of young people. The hardest part for me was when I asked them just before lunch, 'How do you feel this is going?' and got absolutely no feedback. At the end of the workshop I got some positive responses on the 'happy sheets'. I personally think these are a waste of time but for some people they seem important. A friend of mine takes great delight in telling me when the delegates have scored him at the top end of the scale. But the most important learning point for me is how to deal with this wall of silence. Is it that teachers are just low reactors? Potentially, this has the effect of really undermining my confidence. As a mentor, for me it is important to be in tune with what the mentee is thinking about what's going on between us. If I'm not helping I need to know. I can see there is some insecurity on my part when I ask, 'How are you finding this?' but I need to know for both our sakes.

Hull, 12–13 November 1998

I was a facilitator on a management skills programme run on behalf of a unit of a well-known manufacturing company. I loved every minute of the programme. My job, like the other two facilitators, was to give feedback to two delegates who were involved in three role plays over the two-day programme. The delegates ran meetings or one-to-one sessions, such as appraisal opposite a subordinate who each time was played by a professional actor. In the past I used role plays on courses or workshops to help develop skills or bring out key learning points. Latterly, I've almost completely avoided using them. Perhaps I got fed up with hearing from some delegates, 'This isn't a real situation. I'm no good at acting.' On this latest programme I have to say that the actors were superb; they stayed in role during the feedback session and expressed clearly what it was like for them in each given situation. This use of professional actors was a new experience for me and on this particular programme it worked exceptionally well.

Before this I would have said that role playing would not work if you were developing mentoring skills. I always think the 'here and now' is much easier to work with. I haven't necessarily changed my mind about role plays but it's given me some food for thought.

Sheffield, 10 December 1998

I can best sum this up with, 'You win some. You lose some.'

The manager and I spoke to Dave, the apprentice in a fatherly way. This happened on more than one occasion but the message we were trying to get across ran something like this:

> 'Look, Dave you need to work with the craftsmen. It's no good you being constantly cheeky to them. If you want to become a good craftsman you have to listen to them, watch what they do and try things out for yourself. Your future depends quite a lot on the help they are prepared to give you. If you choose to ignore them or continue to be rude to them, there's only one loser.'

Dave seemed to listen to what we had said and agreed to work with the other men rather than against them.

Two days later the manager came to me with a piece of paper that Dave had nailed to the craftsmen's cabin. It said succinctly: 'I'm off on holiday till next week. You lot can all go and … yourselves'. OK so the 'soft' counselling/ mentoring approach doesn't work every time!

Sheffield, 26 January 1999

This group consisting of five or six people (all men and more or less all operating in the same training/consultancy field) has been meeting since 1986. On average we meet once a month and there is no fixed agenda. It has been about sharing thoughts and feelings, avoiding pre-judgements with plenty of unconditional listening. It has not really been about developing work opportunities although at some time or other all the group have met each other on a one-to-one basis and in some cases have worked on joint projects. It is a highly supportive group that has stood the test of time.

On this day, however, I felt I needed to move on and, for the time being at least said I would not be going to any more meetings. I didn't have any disagreement with anyone in the group but just felt, for me at least, that a bit of the magic had gone from our meetings. I suppose it was a form of peer mentoring and it was like bringing a one-to-one mentoring relationship to an end.

I didn't feel any great sadness. This surprises me.

Bridlington, 27–28 February 1999

Although I've run a lot of training courses, I can still feel quite uneasy when I'm attending one myself. I did enjoy the weekend and got some real benefit from it. While I was familiar with most of the mentoring material, I particularly liked Allan's use of nine questions centred around the Kolb model, to identify our preferred learning styles. It was a well handled, relaxing course that in effect modelled a mentoring/counselling like approach.

The key question for me was whether or not I have the aptitude to mentor young people. So, I can probably work quite well in one-to-one situations with most adults, but what about working with a 15-year old? Is the age gap too much of a barrier? I came away thinking I would have a good crack at it, given the opportunity.

After the matching process in March at the school, my first meeting with my mentee took place on March 19.

Sheffield, 5 May 1999

This was my eighth meeting with Bob. He is working on this programme to transform a traditional Sheffield manufacturing company. Consultants are helping him with the programme but he has an exceptionally difficult job. He is intelligent, very personable and seems to have all the right sort of attributes to succeed. He is a good starter with plenty of good ideas but has self-doubts as to his own staying power.

The last time we met I came in on the tail end of a management meeting which he was chairing. It was a review of some very recent communication meetings where some unpalatable news had been given. Afterwards I told Bob that he ran the meeting really well and that his team seemed to be responding very well.

We also reviewed some targets agreed at our previous meeting three weeks earlier. While he seemed to be making considerable strides in communicating change and making various things happen, like selecting a new management team, not much progress seemed to have been made with the targets established at our previous meeting. I didn't feel too concerned about this because overall a hell of a lot of progress seemed to have been made in some difficult areas. Bob felt a bit dissatisfied with himself, however, and said maybe I was letting him off the hook too easily.

I should plan things a bit better, have more options up my sleeve and challenge more.

Rotherham, 18 May 1999

I feel the mentoring I am doing with Sam from the Rotherham school is working out reasonably well. We've had a few meetings and not worked with any sort of agenda. It starts, 'How are you, what have you been doing?' and goes on from there.

I was really interested when someone from the school came to monitor his Trident (work experience) placement at the same time as we were talking together. This person was very nice but I noticed a difference in the way she spoke to him. It differed from my style and while the tone was very friendly, I sensed very much an adult-to-child approach.

Next time I'll check this out with Sam and find out if he thinks I talk to him differently. After the training at Bridlington I wondered if the age gap would be too much for me to mentor effectively.

Sheffield, 19 May 99

My comments at my last meeting with Bob were about my need to challenge him a bit more and also to spend slightly more time on preparation. There was an article on mentoring in *The Sunday Times* about a month ago which said how much time both mentors and mentees should actually spend in preparation before each mentoring session and also the mentee going away each time thinking, 'How dare he say that to me?' This was executive mentoring and I have to say both comments make me think what pretentious crap this was. The point I'm getting to is that this time I did think more about the session in advance and was prepared to challenge Bob more. So, I'd got all these neatly typed notes and was prepared for an interesting session.

Plans of mice and men and all that because when I arrived Bob was about to go into a meeting with his managers and was very pre-occupied with events of this particular day. I went into the meeting and again was impressed with the way Bob ran it and the positive responses he was getting from his managers.

We did manage a quick review of the key targets agreed from the previous meeting. He seemed to have done some of the things since the last meeting, particularly getting out on the shop floor but it was all very rushed. Bob seems to be handling a lot of the difficult, pressure situations quite well. It's good to see this. It would be good for my feelings if I could say this was down to good mentoring but it would be a lie to claim that. I think I've helped him but I'm not sure. The sort of doubts that I reckon are typical for most mentors at some time or other.

Sheffield, May 1998–May 1999

I worked here on and off much longer than originally envisaged. It's mostly been very enjoyable, I've gone back to my personnel roots and the people for the most part have been very easy to get on with. The questions going through my mind have been, 'Do they need mentoring and if so when would be the right time?'

I think, on the one hand, some managers feel isolated and would like some support. Conversely, there's this hard culture which is saying, 'We don't want any of this soft stuff.'

I'm not sure where mentoring and total quality figure in this. Can you have a need for mentoring as a result of TQ? As an organization they've reached the stage where quality teams have been mostly working effectively with some good projects. In terms of the internal customer/supplier chain, they seem to have a long way to go.

I would like to put some form of mentoring in, which would include myself and one other person. Perhaps the target would be about four to five managers initially. One stumbling block is that I haven't sold the idea of mentoring at a high enough level in the organization.

Personal reflections 2

Why do we find self-development processes so difficult?

Most people experience learning as something that is done to them by others rather than something they can control and provide for themselves. From our earliest experiences at school to our first day at work, somebody else determines what we need to know and learn and provides the processes and materials to enable this learning to take place. Both at school and at work we can be punished if we do not comply with the learning process or if we ignore or fail to apply the learning in the appropriate way at the appropriate time.

How unlike our early learning days as an infant, toddler and pre-school child.

During this phase of our development, the whole world was one large adventure playground of self-development and self-discovery. During this phase we touched, tasted, crawled and walked our way through every facet of our limited environment and for the most part thoroughly enjoyed the experience.

Sometimes, on these early journeys of self-development and self-discovery, we felt pain, or anger or hurt. For example, when we touched something hot or sharp; when we tasted something sour or salty; when we landed with a bump the first few times we tried to stand or walk; when we thought we were being left. Usually a concerned adult was on hand to soothe the pain, to reassure us that all was well and to encourage us to try again or not, as the case may be.

At this stage of our development our curiosity and desire for self-discovery and new experiences is still so strong that we do try again and again until we have fully learnt what every lesson was there for us. We learn to learn and grow from our experiences.

It, therefore, seems very sad that, during the formal and compulsory phase of our learning and development, the process of stifling our natural curiosity begins and our voyage of self-discovery is transferred to the tracks of dictated learning.

It is hardly surprising, then, that as adults, we find it very difficult to embrace a process of self-managed, self-determined learning and development like mentoring.

Mentoring is not a process that is done to us by others. It is a process of self-determined learning where we are encouraged to use our own experiences, successes and failures to learn the lessons to ensure our future growth and development.

The role of the mentor in this process is to assist us to see the lessons we can learn from our own experiences and not from the experiences of others. In this way mentoring can and does become our journey of self-discovery.

Mentoring – a change management process

Today more than ever before the only constant we have is *change*:

- the changing of the seasons
- the change from day into night
- growing from infancy to childhood to teenager to young adult to old adult
- changes in technology, learning, and so on.

As people we can and do accept the inevitability of these changes and we adapt and alter our thinking and way of life to accommodate them. Most of the time we do it without thinking.

So why then do we fear at work what is a natural everyday occurrence? Why in the workplace do we constantly try to copy King Canute holding back the wave, or behave like the proverbial ostrich, burying our head in the sand hoping the changes will go away?

If we must copy anyone why not copy nature accepting and adapting to these natural evolutionary processes.

Managing the fear of change

Fear and fear of the unknown are the things that prevent or hold most people back in the change process. Most of this fear comes from internal anxieties rather than external obstacles.

Within the process we feel powerless so we end up exercising our greatest power – *the power to do nothing*.

However, in every situation we always have the power to make four choices:

1   stay with it and stay quiet
2   work to change systems, procedures or the environment
3   get out
4   work to change myself and/or others.

Whatever the situation, either in our work life or our personal life, we always have these four choices.

When shown these choices, most people say that they will 'stay with it and stay quiet' because it appears to be the easiest option. It fact it the hardest because it means if you are not prepared to try to change anything or anyone then you have no right to complain, you have chosen not to change *and* not to say anything about it.

When we accept that we have power in every situation in our life and that we always have these four choices, then the fear of change can and does diminish. We can then begin to explore the realities and practicalities of each of these choices and make decisions accordingly.

These four choices also help us to analyse our *areas of concern* and help us to explore our *range of influence*. We can do this by asking ourselves some simple but key questions:

1   Areas of concern: What are my concerns? Why are they my concerns? Am I prepared to take some actions to begin to eliminate any or all of these concerns?
2   Range of influence: How many of these concerns can I influence? How many of these concerns can I influence with the help and support of others? How many of these concerns are beyond my range of influence at the present time? If I cannot influence these concerns, do I still want to give them my time and energy?

As mentors we can work with and help our mentees to analyse their areas of concern and to explore their ranges of influence. The key questions for the mentee are:

● What can I do differently or better?
● What can we do differently or better?
● What do we need others to do differently or better?
● What help and support do I, we, they need to do it differently or better?
● Where and when will I, we, they get this help and support?

Conclusion

Mentoring can be an effective tool and process for managing both our own self-development and the process of change. Both activities require us to take some control over our own destiny by learning to:

- accept and apply choices as well as
- analysing individual and collective areas of concerns
- exploring individual and collective ranges of influences.

We can *all* learn to conquer our fears and start to become more positive about change and how we manage change and our own self-development.

Recommended reading

Buzan, Tony, *The Mind Map Book*, London: BBC Books, 1993.

Clutterbuck, David, *Counselling Adults – Making the Most of Mentoring*, London: Channel 4 Television, 1995.

Clutterbuck, David, *Everyone Needs a Mentor*, London, IPM Books, 1995.

Coates, Jonathan, *Managing Upwards*, Aldershot: Gower, 1994.

Covey, Steven R., *The Seven Habits of Highly Effective People*, London: Simon & Schuster, 1992.

Fletcher, Barry, Bell, Ann, Buttery, John, Whittaker, Mike, *50 Activities for Achieving Change*, Aldershot, Gower, 1992.

Hagemann, Gisela, *The Motivation Manual*, Aldershot: Gower, 1992.

Handy, Charles, *The Empty Raincoat*, London: Century, 1994.

Holloway, Ann and White, Cathy, *Mentoring The Definitive Workbook*, Swansea: Swansea College, 1995.

Honey, Peter and Mumford Alan, *The Manual of Learning Styles*, 3rd edn, London: Honey, 1992.

Jefferies, Susan, *Feel the Fear and Do It Anyway*, London: Century, 1996.

MacLennan, Nigel, *Coaching and Mentoring*, Aldershot: Gower, 1995.

Megginson, Dave and Clutterbuck, David, *Mentoring in Action*, London: Kogan Page, 1995.

Megginson, Dave and Boydell, Tom, *A Manager's Guide to Coaching*, Bacie, 1979.

Brockbank, Anne and Beech, Nic, *People Management*, 6 May 1999.

Peters, Thomas J. and Waterman Jnr, Robert, *In Search of Excellence*: New York, Harper and Row, 1982.

Rogers, Carl, *Carl Rogers on Personal Power*, London: Constable, 1978.

Rogers, Carl, *Client-Centred Therapy*, London: Century, 1965.

Rogers, Carl, *On Becoming a Person*, London: Constable, 1961.

Stewart, Valerie and Stewart Andrew, *Managing The Poor Performer*, Aldershot: Gower, 1982.

Woodcock, Mike, *Team Development Manual*, 2nd edn, Aldershot: Gower, 1989.

Whittaker, Mike and Cartwright, Ann, *32 Activities on Coaching and Mentoring*, Aldershot, Gower, 1997.

Index

90 Brain Teasers for Trainers

Graham Roberts-Phelps and Anne McDougall

The activities and exercises in this collection are designed to broaden perception, and improve learning, thinking and problem-solving skills. Using them is also a valuable way to boost energy levels at the beginning, middle or end of any training session.

The collection will help any group engage all five senses in their learning, and develop creative and lateral thinking, word usage, mental dexterity and cooperative team skills. Most of the activities require no more than a flip chart or OHP to run. And because they need only a few moments preparation, they can be planned into sessions in advance, or simply introduced to fill gaps, or to signal a change of direction, as appropriate.

Trainers, teachers and team leaders will find *Brain Teasers for Trainers* a rich source of simple, flexible, and easy-to-use exercises, as well as the inspiration for their own variants.

Gower

The Complete Feedback Skills Training Book

Sue Bishop

Feedback is the single most important skill that any manager can use for developing their people. It's also, for many managers, a process with which they are very unfamiliar, and often uncomfortable.

Sue Bishop's *The Complete Feedback Skills Training Book* provides – as the title suggests – a complete range of training and development materials to help managers understand and practise the skills of giving and receiving feedback. It can be used as a resource by trainers, who are developing managers and staff, or as a self-development book for developers themselves.

The book is divided into two parts. Part I, 'Feedback Principles', looks at the generic skills involved, such as learning how to listen, question, understand, accept or reject feedback; how to learn from role models, and how to build and maintain rapport.

Part II, entitled 'Applications', explores how to apply these skills in a variety of management contexts. As feedback is such a universally relevant skill, the author covers all of the most common situations where feedback skills are most useful. These range from the formal, appraisal or selection interviewing, to less formal situations such as coaching or counselling. Whilst most of the advice and exercises focus on one-to-one feedback, there's also a chapter on the manager and teams that explores feedback in a group.

The 20 chapters contain a variety of exercises and activities that include individual and group work, discussion topics, questionnaires, case studies, skills practice and role plays. Each section has a narrative introduction which can be used as an aide memoire for anyone using the manual for self-development.

Sue Bishop's authoritative and highly practical guide will help raise the awareness and 'status' of feedback skills amongst managers as well as providing them with the means and opportunity to reflect on and practise their skills in almost any context.

Gower

Dictionary of HRD

Angus Reynolds, Sally Sambrook and Jim Stewart

Providing succinct definitions of over 3,000 terms. *Dictionary of HRD* is the most comprehensive work of its kind.

Based on Angus Reynolds' successful American dictionary, this new version by Sally Sambrook and Jim Stewart has been extensively reworked with a British and international readership in mind. The entries have been structured to meet the needs of the busy practitioner: definitions of theory are here, but the overall emphasis is on practice. Useful general business terms, which the professional would naturally encounter during the course of their work, are included too.

The Dictionary is organized as follows:

• Over 3,000 terms, arranged alphabetically. Definitions range from a succinct sentence, to a paragraph, depending on significance
• A list of '100 essential HRD terms'
• A list of acronyms and abbreviations
• A list of journals of interest to HRD specialists.

As well as being an invaluable source of reference and new ideas for training and HR professionals and academics, this will be welcomed by a much wider range of managers as an authoritative guide to HR issues, organizations and terminology.

Gower

Evaluating Training

A Resource for Measuring the Results and Impact of Training on People, Departments and Organizations

Sharon Bartram and Brenda Gibson

Training without evaluation is like travelling without a destination. Today's trainers need to demonstrate that what they are doing produces a benefit to the organization that employs them.

Sharon Bartram and Brenda Gibson, authors of the highly successful *Training Needs Analysis*, have turned their attention to the equally important issue of evaluation. They maintain that, by measuring both the results of the learning that takes place and its effect on individuals, departments and organizations, trainers can help people to change their everyday behaviour. And the more you evaluate, the closer you come to creating an environment where learning is a natural part of everyone's routine.

This manual provides a variety of tools and techniques for measuring results. Part One introduces the idea of the evaluation audit. It examines factors such as organizational culture, readiness for learning and evaluation strategy, and shows how to assess current practice and how to plan for the future. Part Two contains 24 instruments for measuring training effectiveness and the impact of training at various levels. They are designed to help you answer two key questions: 'What have people learned?' and 'What difference has their learning made to them, to their department and to the organization?' The forms in Part Two can be copied for immediate use or adapted to suit the needs of your own organization.

Evaluating Training can be used as a means of personal development for trainers; to establish a systematic approach to training evaluation, and as a basis for reviewing whatever evaluation you already undertake.

Whether you are new to evaluation or an 'old hand', you will find much to help you here.

Gower

The Excellent Trainer

Putting NLP to Work

Di Kamp

Most trainers are familiar with the principles of Neuro-Linguistic Programming. What Di Kamp does in her latest book is to show how NLP techniques can be directly applied to the business of training.

Kamp looks first at the fast-changing organizational world in which trainers now operate, then at the role of the trainer and the skills and qualities required. She goes on to deal with the actual training process and provides systematic guidance on using NLP in preparation, delivery and follow-up. Finally she explores the need for continuous improvement, offering not only ideas and explanation but also instruments and activities designed to enhance both personal and professional development.

If you are involved in training, you'll find this book a powerful tool both for developing yourself and for enriching the learning opportunities you create for others.

Gower

Gower Handbook of Training and Development

Third Edition

Edited by Anthony Landale

It is now crystal clear that, in today's ever-changing world, an organization's very survival depends upon how it supports its people to learn and keep on learning. Of course this new imperative has considerable implications for trainers who are now playing an increasingly critical role in supporting individuals, teams and business management. In this respect today's trainers may need to be more than excellent presenters; they are also likely to require a range of consultancy and coaching skills, to understand the place of technology in supporting learning and be able to align personal development values with business objectives.

This brand new edition of the *Gower Handbook of Training and Development* will be an invaluable aid for today's training professional as they face up to the organizational challenges presented to them. All 38 chapters in this edition are new and many of the contributors, whilst being best-selling authors or established industry figures, are appearing for the first time in this form. Edited by Anthony Landale, this *Handbook* builds on the foundations that previous editions have laid down whilst, at the same time, highlighting many of the very latest advances in the industry.

The *Handbook* is divided into five sections - learning organization, best practice, advanced techniques in training and development, the use of IT in learning, and evaluation issues.

Gower

A Handbook for Training Strategy

Second Edition

Martyn Sloman

When the first edition of Martyn Sloman's *Handbook* appeared in 1994, it made an immediate impact on the HRD community. Its starting point was the idea that traditional approaches to training in the organization were no longer effective. The *Handbook* introduced a new model and set out the practical implications.

The world of HRD has moved on, and Martyn Sloman has now drastically revised the text to reflect the increased complexity of organizational life and the many recent developments in the field. His aim remains the same: to help readers to develop a framework in which training can be effectively managed and delivered.

In Part I of the text the author draws attention to the opportunities created for training by the current emphasis on competition through people. In Part II he poses the question: 'What should training managers be doing to ensure that training in their organization is as good as it can be?' Here he stresses the need to keep training aligned with business objectives, and to encourage line managers to work alongside the human resource professionals. The third and final Part considers the trainer as a strategic facilitator and examines the skills required.

Martyn Sloman writes as an experienced training manager and his book is concerned, above all, with implementation. Thus the text is supported by questionnaires, survey instruments and specimen documents. With its combination of thought-provoking argument and practical guidance, the *Handbook* will continue to serve all those with an interest in organizational training.

Gower

How to Deliver Training

Martin Orridge

'The aim of this book is to provide both managers wishing to run 'in team' exercises and those entering the training profession with a practical guide to delivering successful developmental events', says Martin Orridge in the Preface.

He writes as an experienced trainer and consultant, producing a very human guide to the realities of running a training event. In a brief introductory section he explains the need for training and the benefits it can bring. Part 1 of the main text shows how to design a successful training session and Part 2 deals in detail with preparation and delivery. At the end is a collection of model documents and forms that can be used at various stages of the training cycle. The text includes tips, tools, checklists, examples and exercises throughout, together with real-life anecdotal 'cameos' to help make the points memorable.

Martin Orridge's style is at all times practical and friendly. *How to Deliver Training* will be welcomed not only by professional trainers, but by all managers and team leaders concerned with staff development.

Gower

Web-Based Training

Colin Steed

Web-based training is becoming one of the most important tools for trainers and courseware developers. The ability to deliver training and learning online to an individual's desk offers enormous flexibility for the organization as well as the employee, cost and time savings and the opportunity to keep pace with constant changes required for today's organizations to remain competitive.

Colin Steed explains how trainers can use self-paced, online learning to develop and train employees and improve their performance. He outlines the benefits and drawbacks of web-based training, looks at the cost considerations, and examines the elements that make up a programme. There is plenty of coverage of what is currently available on the market as well as in-depth case material drawn from organizations that have already begun to use the technology. Using step-by-step procedures, and assuming no technical knowledge, this practical and timely book will help you design your own web-based training strategy.

If you want to know what web-based training is all about and whether it's right for your organization, this book provides all the answers.

Gower